YORKSHIRE'S PAST FROM THE AIR

Edited by D. N. Riley

for the Aerial Archaeology Committee of the Yorkshire Archaeological Society

published by
Sheffield Academic Press
for the Yorkshire Archaeological Society

Yorkshire's Past from the Air

edited by D.N. Riley

Sheffield Academic Press

Published by
Sheffield Academic Press Ltd
The University of Sheffield
343 Fulwood Road
Sheffield S10 3BP
England

Typeset by Sheffield Academic Press
and
printed in Great Britain
by Billing & Sons Ltd
Worcester

British Library Cataloguing in Publication Data available

ISBN 1-85075-130-7

LIST OF SITES DESCRIBED

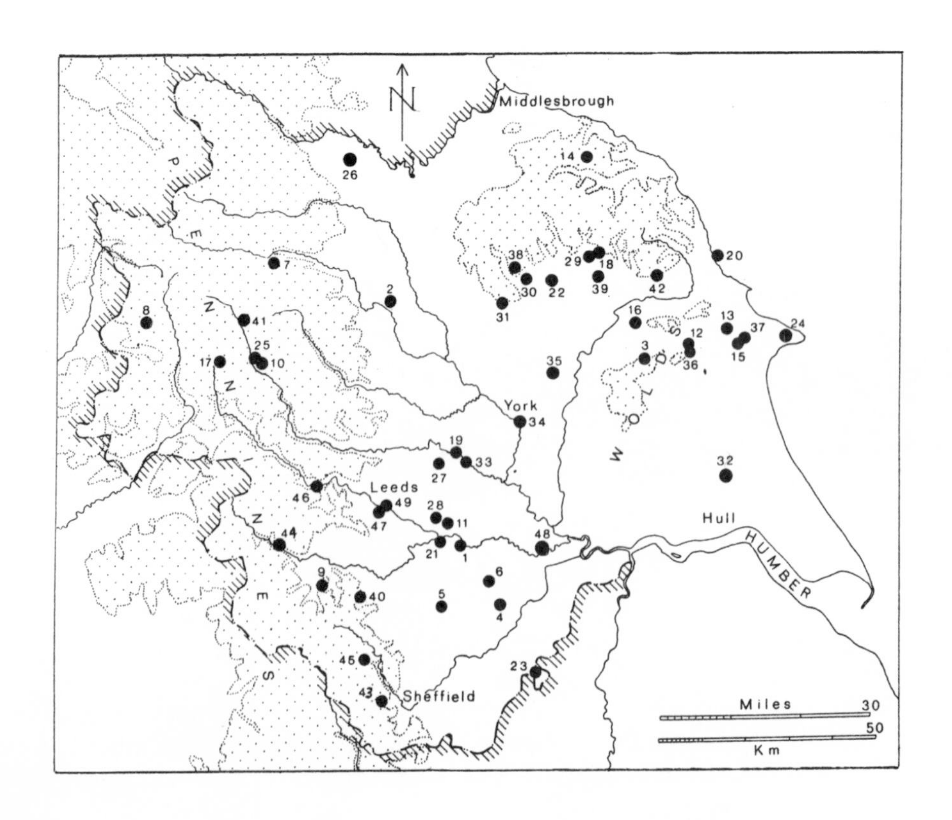
N
Middlesbrough
York
Leeds
Hull
HUMBER
Sheffield
Miles 30
Km 50

INTRODUCTION

Invention hence her compasse steeres,
Towards Yorke the most renown'd of Shires,
Makes the three Ridings in their Stories,
Each severally to shew their glories.

From *Poly-Olbion* by Michael Drayton [1563-1631].

The splendid landscape of Yorkshire includes many different types of country: the high moors of the uplands in the north and west, the broad acres of the Vales of York and Pickering, and the rolling hills of the Wolds. Everywhere there are sights which remind us of the past achievements of Yorkshiremen. Some of these are familiar to everyone who lives in the region, York Minster, for example, but few people realize how much more can be seen from a light aircraft flying at a height of one or two thousand feet. Taking advantage of the aerial view, archaeologists have received great assistance from photographs of ancient remains invisible or barely visible to observers on the ground, such as the great ring that formerly encircled Duggleby Howe (3). When it was intact, this ring must have been one of the largest early prehistoric monuments in Great Britain. Many other aerial discoveries of prehistoric and Romano-British sites in Yorkshire are given in the first part of this book. From the air, we can also look at well-known places from a new angle and see them as a whole, so that their plans can be appreciated better than is possible from the restricted surface viewpoint. Many views of this kind are given, mainly in the second half of the book, the pictures of York (34) and Saltaire (46) being good examples of the comprehensive aerial view.

The first archaeological air photographs of Yorkshire sites were taken between the wars. They were Royal Air Force photographs of land near Grassington, which were made in response to a suggestion by Dr Arthur Raistrick. The first local archaeologist to take air photographs himself was T.C.M. Brewster, who made some flights over the Wolds in the late 1930s. It was not until after the second world war, however, that systematic aerial exploration and recording took place in the county. Professor J.K. St Joseph then began to make sorties from his base at Cambridge to various parts of England, including many flights over Yorkshire, where he found and recorded a large number of antiquities, nearly all of which were new discoveries. In the 1970s J.N. Hampton of the Air Photographs Unit, National Monuments Record, flying in an aircraft based near London, also made many successful visits to East Yorkshire. Much, however, remained to be done by local archaeologists, who did not need to fly long distances to reach their objective and had the advantage of detailed knowledge of their areas and of the local weather conditions.

In 1972 the Aerial Archaeology Committee of the Yorkshire Archaeological society was formed at the suggestion of T.G. Manby. I was fortunate in being the first locally based archaeologist to receive the backing of the committee as an air photographer, helped by a donation made to the committee by Mrs R. Hartley. New discoveries were made on my first flights, particularly in West and South Yorkshire, which had not received a great deal of attention previously. Later, other Yorkshire archaeologists took to the skies, and at present systematic work is taking place in North, West and South Yorkshire and Humberside. Since the Wolds have already been fairly thoroughly examined, archaeological air survey is in a more advanced state in Yorkshire than in most areas of similar size in this country. With this in mind, Dr P.V. Addyman proposed the present book, to show a little of the results and make the work of the Committee more widely known.

The photographs copied here were almost all taken by members of the Committee. An impression of the parts of the county to which Yorkshire fliers have devoted most attention is given by the map on page 6, which shows the positions of places illustrated. It should be noted that the county boundary shown on the map is that which existed before 1974. This is because the Yorkshire Archaeological Society's concern is the historic county of Yorkshire, composed of the North, East and West Ridings. It is now divided principally between North, South and West Yorkshire and North Humberside. The places photographed tend to be clustered in certain regions, partly as a result of the unusually large number of early remains visible from the air in the northern part of the Wolds and in some of the Dales, and partly because most photographers have spent their time in particular areas, for example A.L. Pacitto in the north-east and Dr R.E. Yarwood in the modern county of West Yorkshire. In a few cases it was found that the places chosen were shown better by Cambridge photographs, which have been reproduced instead, with permission from the University Committee for Aerial Photography. The large areas on the map from which there are no photographs in the book are of course mainly the result of the small number which can be reproduced in a work of this kind—the total number of archaeological photographs taken from the air over the county runs into tens of thousands.

The main objectives of archaeologists during their reconnaissance flights have been the discovery and recording of previously unknown ancient sites, in which, as already stated, they have been very successful. In most cases the photography of old towns and buildings and the familiar sights of the historic landscape of Yorkshire has been a secondary purpose. A balance must be struck in the choice of subjects, and it is easy to err in one direction or the other because so much often demands attention. From the height of one or two thousand feet the ground appears to pass by fairly slowly, but, as the aircraft is flying at a speed of about one hundred miles per hour, nothing stays in view for very long. I must confess to having very often concentrated my attention so much on the search for the frequently faint traces of prehistoric and Romano-British sites, that I have missed many opportunities of taking beautiful pictures like that of Helmsley Castle (30). It is therefore a good thing that some of the other photographers, e.g. Dr R.E. Yarwood in the Leeds area, have given much more attention to townscapes and landscapes.

Prints of the illustrations given here are included in the collection of about five thousand air photographs stored in the library of the Yorkshire Archaeological Society at Claremont, Clarendon Road, Leeds. The collection, which is being added to every year, is available for consultation by members. Larger numbers of photographs are stored in the libraries of the University Committee for Aerial Photography in Cambridge and of the Air Photography Unit, National Monuments Record in London.

The photography of buildings or landscapes from the air is not difficult for any competent photographer, providing that he takes pains to overcome the problems of work in this situation. The search for ancient sites visible only from the air is, however, something different. The ways in which they appear, by shadows, soil marks and crop marks, or at times by other means, are familiar to most archaeologists, but as this book is intended for a wider circle of readers, some explanation of these terms is necessary.

The shadows thrown by the sun when low in the sky are an important aid in the study of slight earthworks. The Roman marching camp at Malham (17) is illustrated under the light of the evening sun, with the help of which the low banks of the camp are easily traceable on the ground. Several other inconspicuous earthworks (25 and 36–38) are seen under a similar low light. Such places are sometimes called *shadow sites*. They may be old mounds, banks and ditches, or else the remains of ruined walls that have been grassed over in the course of centuries. Sometimes, however, the stones of old walls may be still on the surface, for example at the settlement site on Penhill (7), where they appear as light lines, contrasting with the darker tone of the surrounding grass. In such cases, the ancient features show well without the need for shadows to emphasize them.

When land on which there are ancient earthworks is ploughed for the first time, the colour of the ploughed soil generally give the positions of former banks as light coloured lines, and ditches or hollows as dark coloured. *Soil marks*, as they are usually called, are seen at several sites (1, 4A and 36A). They may reveal the site plans very clearly, though it is very unusual to see them as well as on the medieval village site at Cowlam (36A). There the marks were exceptionally distinct because the remains of low walls of chalk blocks were brought to the surface by the plough. Soil marks are unfortunately often signs that ancient remains are being destroyed (4A). They may also result from natural variations of soil composition and from modern disturbances of the ground, such as those caused by gas pipelines; photographs must therefore always be interpreted with a knowledge of the landscape. After some years of cultivation of a field, soil marks are spread by ploughing, become faint, and finally disappear because of the mixing of the soil. Marks in soil above chalk last much longer than those in other soils, so there are many more marks to be seen on the chalky soils of the Wolds than elsewhere in Yorkshire.

On the intensively cultivated land that covers much of Yorkshire, the most important sources of information are marks in growing crops, usually termed *crop marks*. They are seen most often in barley and wheat, to a lesser extent in sugar beet, and sometimes in certain other crops. Differences in soil depth are their principal cause, and hence they appear in places where its depth is increased by the fillings of ancient pits and ditches (15). The growth of crops is, however, a complex matter that is influenced by many factors. Some types of soil are favourable to the development of marks in crops growing in them, for example, thin soils above gravel or chalk, while others, such as clayey soils, are unfavourable. Dry weather in early summer is generally needed for the marks to show well. A number of photographs record crop marks of archaeological importance (1A–3, 5, 6, 11–13, 16, 19 and 23) which clearly differ from marks due to natural causes, such as former watercourses (2 and 19). They must also be distinguished from the frequent marks caused by modern agriculture, e.g. the dark lines known as the 'envelope pattern' (3). Marks due to current farm work normally last for only one year, but the marks of archaeological interest last indefinitely, because the ancient remains that cause them are buried beneath the plough soil.

The contents of this book are arranged more or less in chronological order. The first illustrations show monuments of the Neolithic period, probably dating from the third millennium BC. In spite of their very early date they are of great size (1–3). They are followed by a group of photographs of sites (5–16) which have been allocated with a greater or lesser degree of certainty to the period known as the Bronze Age, dating from the second and early first millennia B.C., and the next period, the Early Iron Age, which lasted until the Roman conquest. They include hillforts, burial mounds, field boundaries and sites generally described as enclosures (5 and 6), which are the ditches dug to enclose settlements or farms, and are difficult to date without excavation. From the frequency of these sites it must be deduced that Yorkshire, and indeed the whole of England, was more densely settled in early times than was formerly thought.

The defences of Roman temporary camps and forts (17–19), with their straight sides and carefully rounded corners, and often their 'playing card' shape, can easily be distinguished from the less regular forms of settlement enclosures. They are a reminder of the arrival of the Roman army in the later first century AD. The life of the local inhabitants, however, probably went on with little change in most places. There is in general little in the appearance of the remains of Romano-British agriculture to distinguish them from the work of the previous period. In Wharfedale, for example, it seems that Romano-British people continued to farm the fields of their Early Iron Age ancestors (10).

There are few distinctive remains that can be attributed directly to the period of the Anglo-Saxon invaders of the fifth century AD and later, although certain linear earthworks probably belong to that time (24). More settled conditions returned in due course and, following the conversion to Christianity, church building began in the seventh and eighth centuries AD at places which are still in use today (26).

We now reach firmer ground when commenting on the photographs. The study of the history of the Middle Ages is based on a wealth of documents that have survived, and many buildings of that period can still be seen, even though often only as ruins (30 and 31). It has been realized in recent years that archaeological excavation, field work and air photography have much to add about the aspects of medieval life that are little known or unknown from documents, in particular the life of the villages, inhabited by the peasant farmers who formed the majority of the population. Low earthworks in many places show the sites of former medieval villages (36 and 37), which have been abandoned and never reoccupied. Villages were deserted for various reasons in the Middle Ages, the most important of which was the replacement of arable farming by sheep. Much land reverted from arable to grass, thus preserving the characteristic strip plan of the medieval and later open fields (32 and 35) which can still be seen as rigg (or ridge) and furrow in many places, though much has been levelled by modern ploughing (39).

In the eighteenth and nineteenth centuries Yorkshire was at the forefront of a movement which later changed the whole world—the Industrial Revolution. We are reminded of some of the activities which lead up to this development by photographs of primitive mines, which were in use from the sixteenth century onwards (40 and 41). Two photographs show places that have a long history of industrial use (43 and 44) and another shows Saltaire (46), one of the most impressive urban developments created by nineteenth century industry. When examined in more detail, the disadvantages of nineteenth century town housing become more apparent, but it must be remembered what a great advance it was from the insanitary conditions of medieval towns. Has a comparable advance been made in the twentieth century? The townscapes also include York (34), a city that has been important in every period from the Roman to the present, and Leeds in 1927 (49), with its surprisingly empty streets at the beginning of the motor age. The latter comes from the library of the Thoresby Society, which has kindly allowed publication.

The descriptions of the photographs have been written by members of the Aerial Archaeology Committee: the prehistoric sites by T.G. Manby, Roman by H.G. Ramm, medieval by Dr L.A.S. Butler and post-medieval by S. Moorhouse. The Committee is grateful for assistance from Dr R.K. Morris and Dr D.A. Spratt, who have written about sites of which they had special knowledge, and to Mrs J. Cass for information about Loxley Valley (43). Photographs showing remains of more than one period have in some cases been described by two contributors.

What do we learn of Yorkshire from the photographs of such a diverse series of places, occupied at various periods for very different purposes? First, how many places may be identified where our early ancestors lived, though often they can only be found now as crop marks, and how much greater the population may have been in prehistoric and Roman times than is generally realized—even allowing for the fact that only a proportion of the ancient settlement sites were in use at any one time. Secondly, how people combined together even at earliest periods to build great structures like the henges seen at Ferrybridge and Thornborough (1 and 2). Thirdly, how extensive was the land cultivated by medieval peasant farmers, whose work supported the builders of the more spectacular remains of the Middle Ages—castles, cathedrals and abbeys. Fourthly, and most important, we see the continuity that runs through English history and the example of great achievement set by our forebears.

D.N. Riley

Note. Drawings have been prepared to help the reader to understand some of the photographs. The features described in the text are shown, together with various modern boundaries, which are marked thus — . — . — . — .

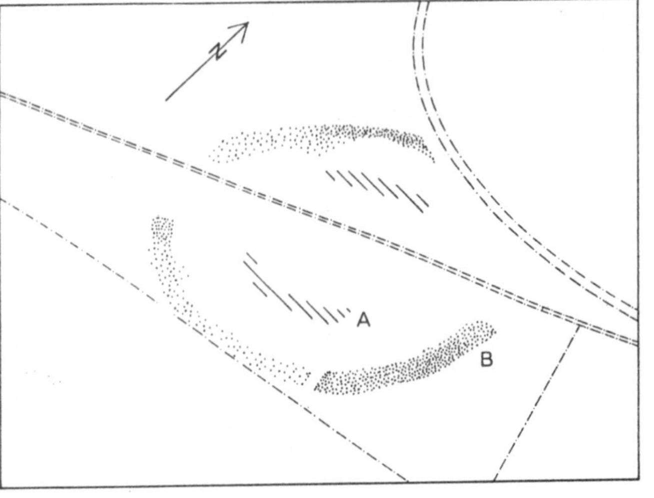

N
A
B

1. NEOLITHIC HENGE MONUMENT: FERRYBRIDGE, WEST YORKSHIRE

(formerly West Riding), SE 474 242

A henge is a neolithic structure, probably built for ritual purposes. The main parts are usually a large circular ditch with a broad bank outside it, and one or two entrances. This large example stands on cultivated land, on which its bank is revealed by a light-toned soil mark (B) where winter ploughing has spread soil from the remains of the earthwork. The destruction of a part of the bank by the realignment of the Castleford to Ferrybridge road is seen clearly. A modern field lane transects the site, running through the two opposed entrances of the henge. The bank is 200 m in diameter, surviving in places to 1 m high and spread by cultivation to a width of 30 m. Within the monument, the broad internal ditch is shown by dark soil (A), but its position is given more distinctly by the crop marks seen on the next photograph (1A).

T.G. Manby

Photograph by D.N. Riley, 24 March 1981
References: J.K. St Joseph, 'Aerial Reconnaissance: Recent Results, 50', *Antiquity* 54 (1980), pp. 132-35

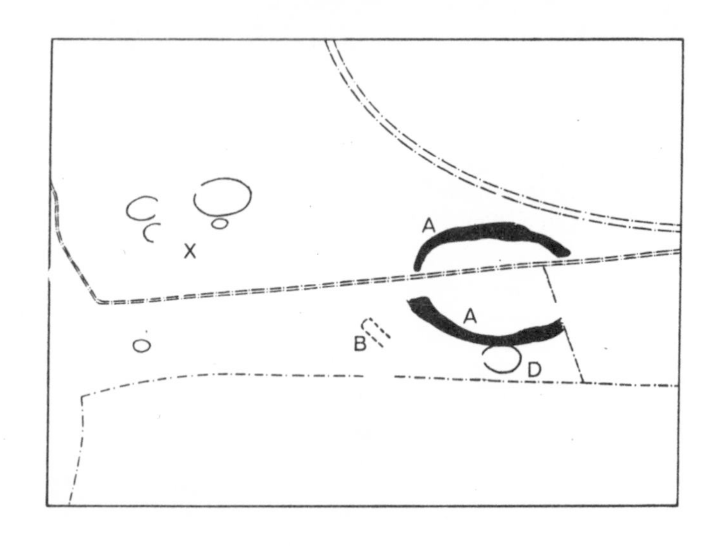

A
X
A
B
D

1A. ANOTHER PHOTOGRAPH OF THE FERRYBRIDGE HENGE

This photograph shows the same site as before, but seen at a different time of the year. In contrast to the winter soil marks on the other photograph, this summer view shows a complementary series of crop marks that contribute to a fuller understanding of the monument. The position of the ditch is given fairly clearly by dark marks (AA), through which are two entrance gaps. The bank hardly shows, except near one of the entrances, where its end is suggested by a dark mark (B). On the left of the picture are several small circular crop marks, which are caused by the features usually termed ring ditches (X), and another ring (D) is very close to the ditch of the henge. These ring ditches probably mark the sites of Bronze Age round barrows or burial mounds, part of a cluster near the henge; one mound survived until the landscaping of the area near the power station in 1962.

T.G. Manby

Photograph by D.N. Riley, 5 August 1981
Reference: A.L. Pacitto, 'The Excavation of Two Bronze Age Burial Mounds at Ferry Fryston in the West Riding of Yorkshire', *Yorkshire Archaeological Journal* 42 (1967-70), pp. 295-305

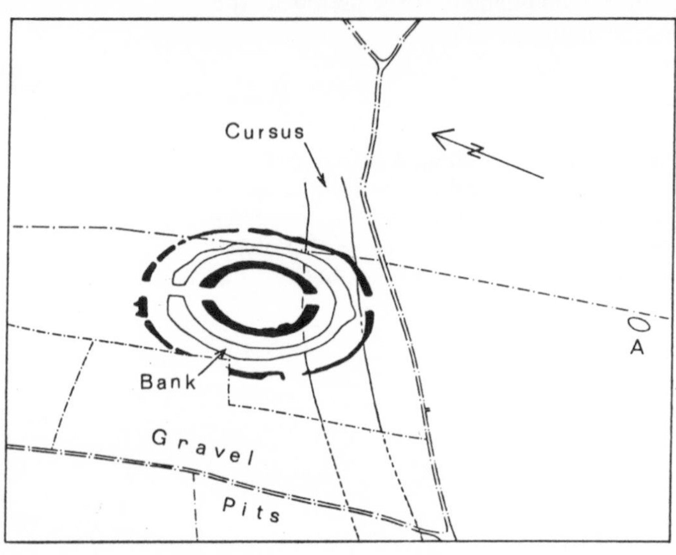
Cursus
Bank
Gravel
Pits
A

2. NEOLITHIC HENGE AND CURSUS MONUMENTS: THORNBOROUGH, NORTH YORKSHIRE

(formerly in North Riding), SE 286 795

The big circular feature is the central henge of the three that stand near Thornborough village. It has a massive bank that is still upstanding, but the rest of the field is under cultivation, and the two accompanying ditches appear as dark crop marks. The marks of the broad internal ditch with its squared terminals at the two entrances contrast with those of the narrow outer ditch with its many causeways.

The henge overlies an earlier monument of the type known as a cursus, the filled-in ditches of which produce two long crop marks running parallel with the modern road to Thornborough village. The purpose of very long Neolithic enclosures of this kind is assumed to have been ceremonial. The name of cursus was given to them by an eighteenth-century archaeologist, who speculated that they were intended for some sacred race or procession (cursus is a Latin word meaning a race or route). The ditches of the cursus were formerly continued to a curved end at a point below the lower edge of the photograph, but that part has now been destroyed by the gravel pit seen in the foreground, which has also impinged on the outer ditch of the henge. The crop mark ring on the right of the photograph (A) gives the site of a former barrow, now ploughed away.

The broad dark marks with curved edges beyond and to the left of the henge are caused by uneven depths of soil covering the gravel that underlies this land. They give the positions of torrential streams that laid down these gravels in the Ice Age.

T.G. Manby

Photograph by D.N. Riley, 10 July 1976

References: W.C. Lukis, 'On the Flint Implements and Tumuli of the Neighbourhood of Wath', *Yorkshire Archaeological Journal* 1 (1870), pp. 116-25

N. Thomas, 'The Thornborough Circles, near Ripon, North Riding', *Yorkshire Archaeological Journal* 38 (1952-55), pp. 425-45.

F. de M. Vatcher, 'Thornborough Cursus, Yorkshire', *Yorkshire Archaeological Journal* 40 (1959-62), pp. 169-82

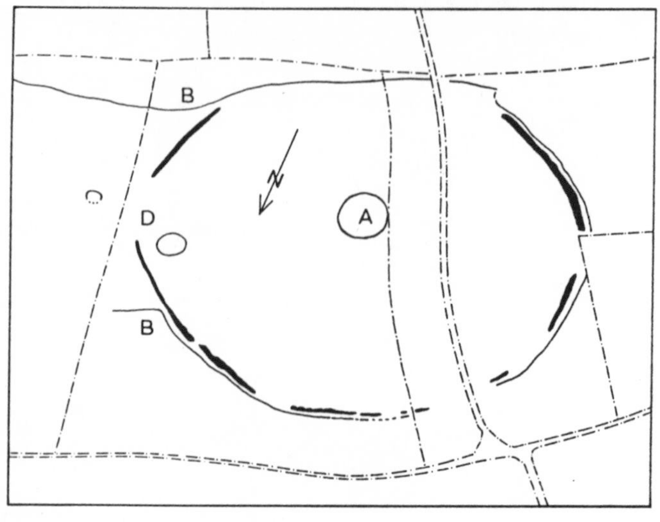
B
D
A
B

3. NEOLITHIC BURIAL MOUND AND ENCLOSURE: DUGGLEBY, NORTH YORKSHIRE

(formerly in East Riding), SE 880669

This photograph shows the site of one of the largest Neolithic monuments in Britain. Duggleby Howe (A), a round barrow of exceptional size, stands on the chalk slope of the Great Wold Valley at the centre of a big ring of crop marks. The size of the Howe and the ring can be judged by comparison with the houses seen at the base of the photograph. A richly furnished series of late Neolithic burials were found when the Howe was partially excavated by J.R. Mortimer in 1890.

We now know from the crop marks that the Howe originally stood in an enclosure about 370 m in diameter, which was encircled by two ditches. They may represent two phases. The broad inner ditch has interruptions; there are wide gaps between its various portions and it does not appear on the uphill part of the circuit (top of photograph). It probably lay inside an external bank and has good parallels in the large Late Neolithic henge monuments of Southern Britain. Close to its eastern side are crop marks of two small ring ditches (D), which may be the sites of round barrows or of ditches enclosing timber structures. The narrow outer ditch of the enclosure is continuous except for a large break on the eastern side, where both ends turn outwards (BB); it was probably made when the monument was incorporated into a divided and controlled landscape of ancient farms. It clearly pre-dates the medieval rigg and furrow cultivation of the area, the plan of which is perpetuated by the curved boundaries (compare 39) of the narrow field between the Howe and the modern road. This later enclosure ditch perhaps marked off the land round the Howe when it was the assembly point for the Domesday Hundred of Torshau (Thor's Howe) or the Wapentake of Buckrose that met at Duggleby in the early Middle Ages.

Dark marks in the crops have also developed at places where farm machinery turned corners during recent cultivation of the field. They form triangles at both ends of the field containing the Howe. Marks of this kind are often seen and are called the 'envelope pattern'.

T.G. Manby

Photograph by D.N. Riley, 8 August 1979

References: J.R. Mortimer, *Forty Years' Researches in British and Saxon Burial Mounds of East Yorkshire* (London, 1905), pp. 23-42
D.N. Riley, 'Recent Air Photographs of Duggleby Howe and the Ferrybridge Henge', *Yorkshire Archaeological Journal* 52 (1980), pp. 174-78
Kinnes, I. et al., 'Duggleby Howe Reconsidered', *Archaeological Journal* 140 (1983), pp. 83-108

4. ENCLOSURES ON SUTTON COMMON, ASKERN, SOUTH YORKSHIRE
(formerly in West Riding), SE 564 121

Two earthwork bank and ditch enclosures stand on low sandhills, surrounded by peat. When this photograph was taken, the wet grassland was used as rough grazing and for hay. The larger earthwork has a double circuit of banks and ditches, the latter segmented, with gaps or causeways between. Excavations made in the 1930s showed that the banks covered wooden palisades; the points of the stakes were preserved by the wet conditions that also preserved a single piece (solid) wooden wheel in a ditch segment. Radiocarbon tests on samples of wood obtained during recent excavations by the South Yorkshire Archaeology Unit have established an Early Iron Age date (early fourth century B.C.) for these enclosures. They had been overwhelmed by peat growth caused by the rising water table of the low lying Humberhead levels. The earthworks emerged after the area was enclosed and drained in the early nineteenth century.

T.G. Manby

Photograph by D.N. Riley, 7 July 1976
Reference: C.E. Whiting, 'Excavations on Sutton Common 1933, 1934 and 1935', *Yorkshire Archaeological Journal* 33 (1936-38), pp. 57-81

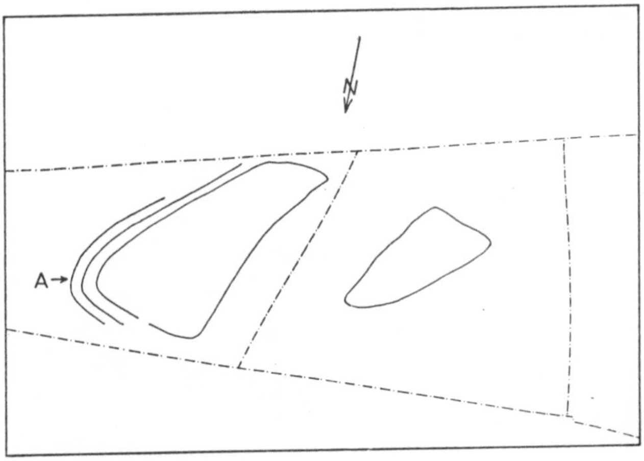

4A. SUTTON COMMON FOUR YEARS LATER

The same site is seen after new access roads have been made and the drainage ditches deepened to lower the water table, thus making arable cultivation possible. The larger eastern enclosure has been ploughed up and its banks levelled. There is now a soil mark on its site, on which the banks and the edge of part of the outer ditch (A) are light toned and the peat fill of the ditches shows dark. Note the serrated appearance of these marks, caused by plough drag. The interior of the ploughed enclosure is light toned because of its sandy surface, but the dark peat shows elsewhere, there being clearly a peat filled hollow between the two earthworks. The western enclosure had not been ploughed at the time of this photograph, but cultivation has since been extended over all the land round it. This is a site of great importance, as the waterlogged peaty deposits preserve wooden and other objects that do not survive in dry ground.

T.G. Manby

Photograph by D.N. Riley, 29 May 1980

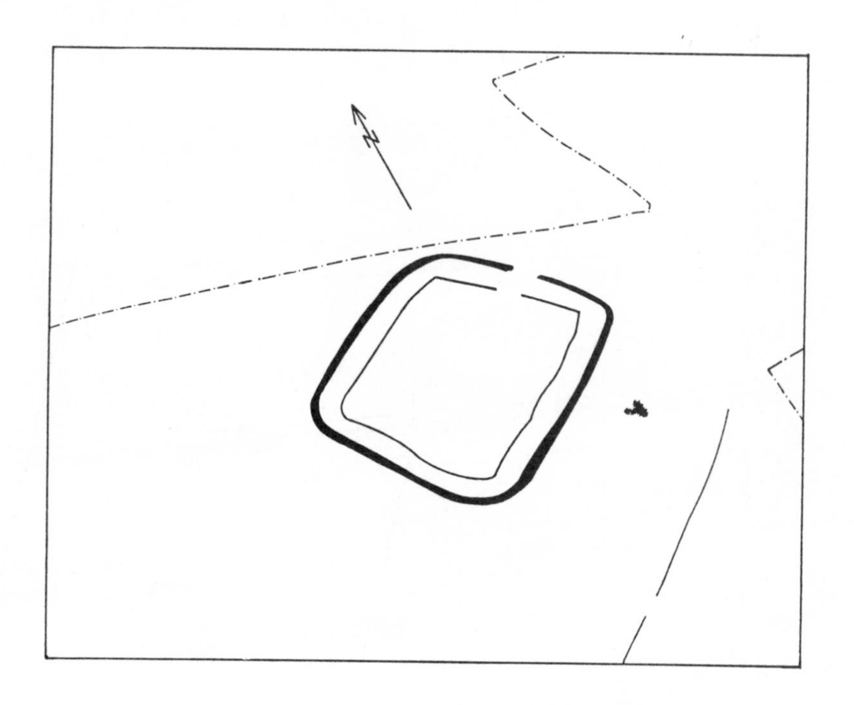

5. DOUBLE DITCHED ENCLOSURE: SOUTH KIRKBY, WEST YORKSHIRE

(formerly in West Riding), SE 429 110

This enclosure is shown by crop marks on soil above sandstone of the Coal Measures series. There are notable contrasts between the two elements seen here; the broad outer mark obviously indicates a filled up ditch, but the inner feature is narrow, with irregular sides and square corners which suggest that it is caused by the foundation trench for a timber palisade. A wide entrance gap on the far side suggests that defence was a secondary consideration when the site was occupied.

Rectangular enclosures of ditches and palisades around farmsteads are known in many periods—the Later Bronze Age, the Early Iron Age and the Romano-British period. Only excavation could determine the date and purpose of this enclosure, which is not accompanied by any visible remains of a system of fields.

T.G. Manby

Photograph by West Yorkshire Archaeology Service (R.E. Yarwood), 29 July 1983

Reference: R.E. Yarwood and J.J. Marriott, *The Aerial Time Machine* (Wakefield, 1988), p. 18

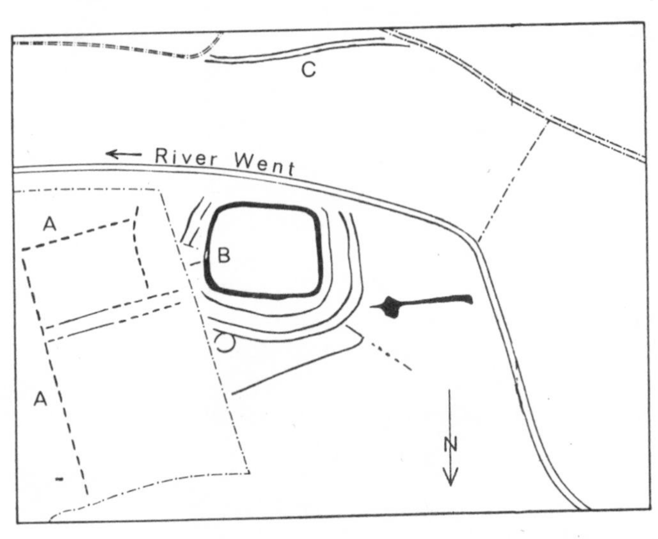
C
River Went
A
B
A
N

6. MULTIPLE DITCHED ENCLOSURE: LITTLE SMEATON, WEST YORKSHIRE

(formerly in West Riding), SE 535 158

Crop marks enclose an area of approximately square shape on sandy soil near the River Went. The entrance appears to have been on the eastern side (B), though the broad innermost ditch shows no definite gap and the three outer ditches are obscured near the modern field boundary. Faint crop marks are seen in the field on the left. More marks (AA), perhaps caused by old field boundaries (shown on the drawing by broken lines), were recorded here in the previous year, when conditions were different. Worked flints of very early (Mesolithic) date have been found in the interior of the enclosure, but a better indication of its period is given by a bronze brooch, probably of first-century AD date recovered during the dredging of the River Went, the canalised course of which skirts the site. The enclosure is large enough to have contained a farmstead, and its surround may not have been as strong as the crop marks suggest, for the ditches may not all have been in use at the same time.

A light band between two darker marks at the top of the photograph shows the former course of part of a road.

T.G. Manby

Photograph by D.N. Riley, 29 July 1979

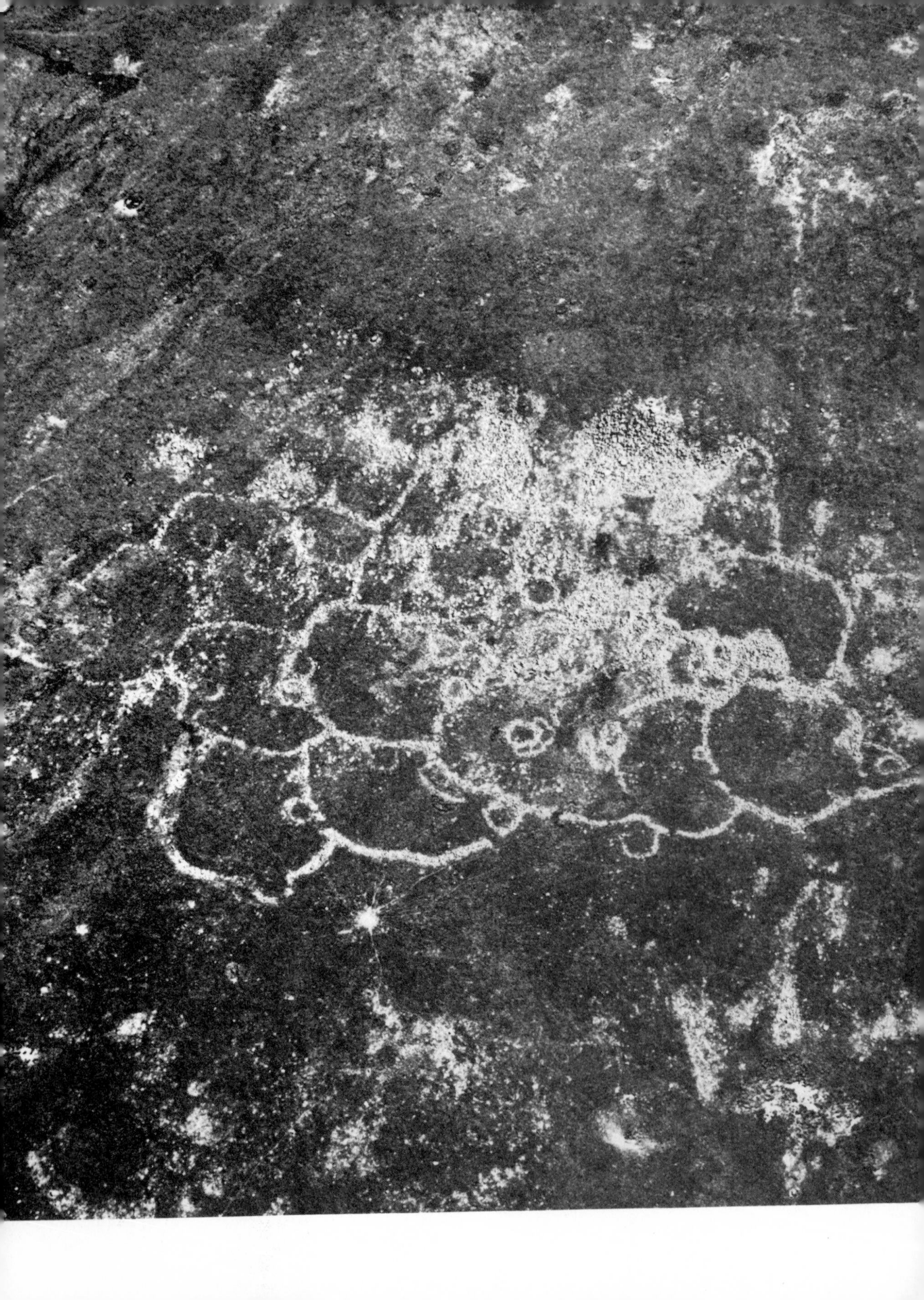

7. STONE WALLED ENCLOSURES AND HUT CIRCLES: WEST BURTON, NORTH YORKSHIRE

(formerly in North Riding), SE 031 860

Tumbled limestone walls stand out amidst the moorland pasture growing on soil above rock of the Yoredale series on the western slopes of Penhill. Ancient structures survive well in areas of the Pennines such as this, which are too remote for stone robbers, and where the only causes of destruction have been the weather and the feet of animals. This site at 1500 ft (450 m) has on its eastern side (top of photograph) a natural terrace which gives some shelter. From a nucleus that includes a ring enclosure around a hut circle, a series of curvilinear walled enclosures appear as if built out successively. Hut circles occur in each enclosure and are commonly incorporated in the enclosure wall. The complex may be of Bronze Age date, with enclosures intended for animals or for gardening; the absence of ancient fields and the altitude suggest that the site was probably used in a stock rearing or a forest economy. The bare landscape of the Pennines today contrasts with the forests that grew there in the Bronze Age, providing shelter and a great variety of environment for exploitation by man.

T.G. Manby

Photograph by D.N. Riley, 17 July 1978

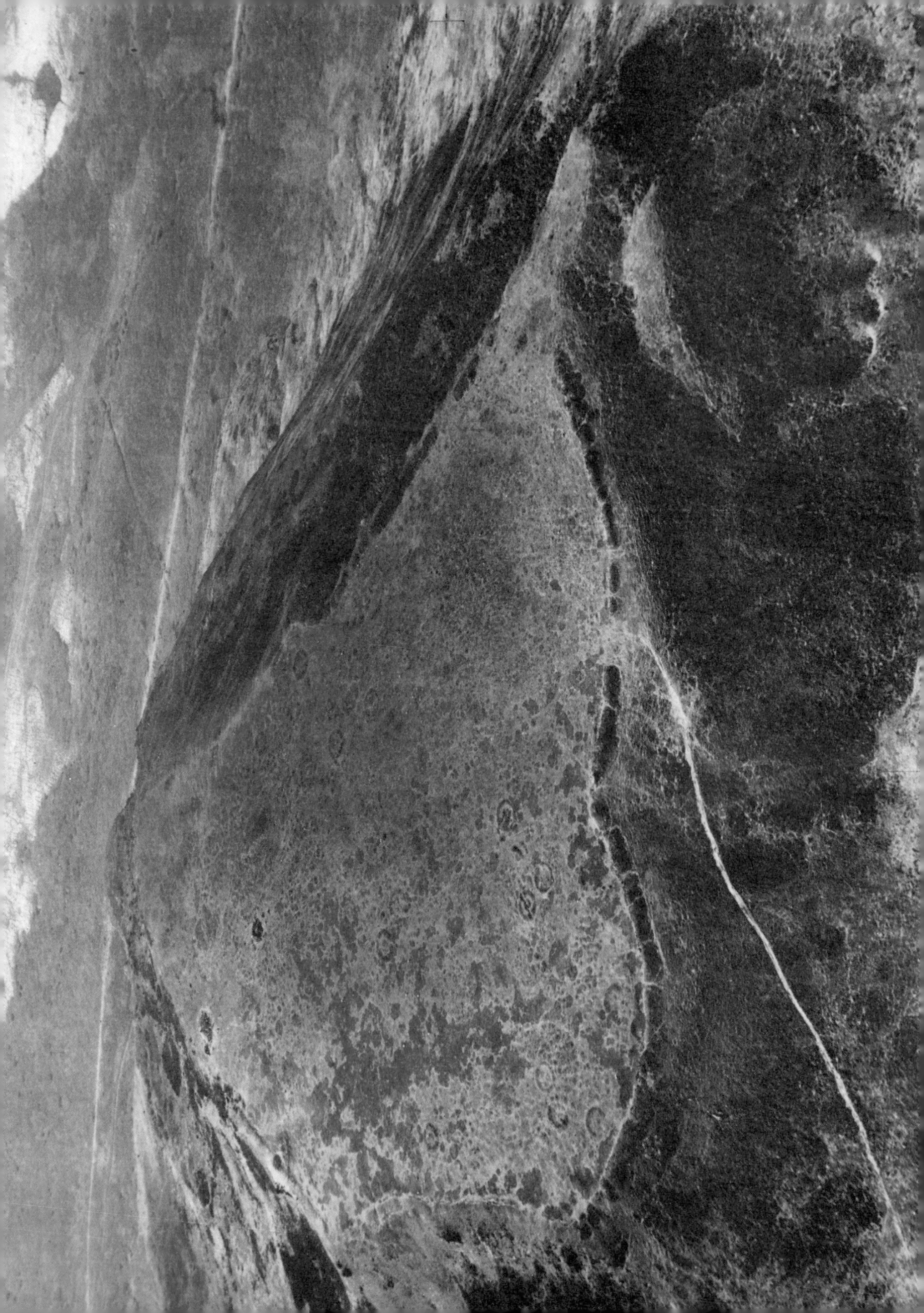

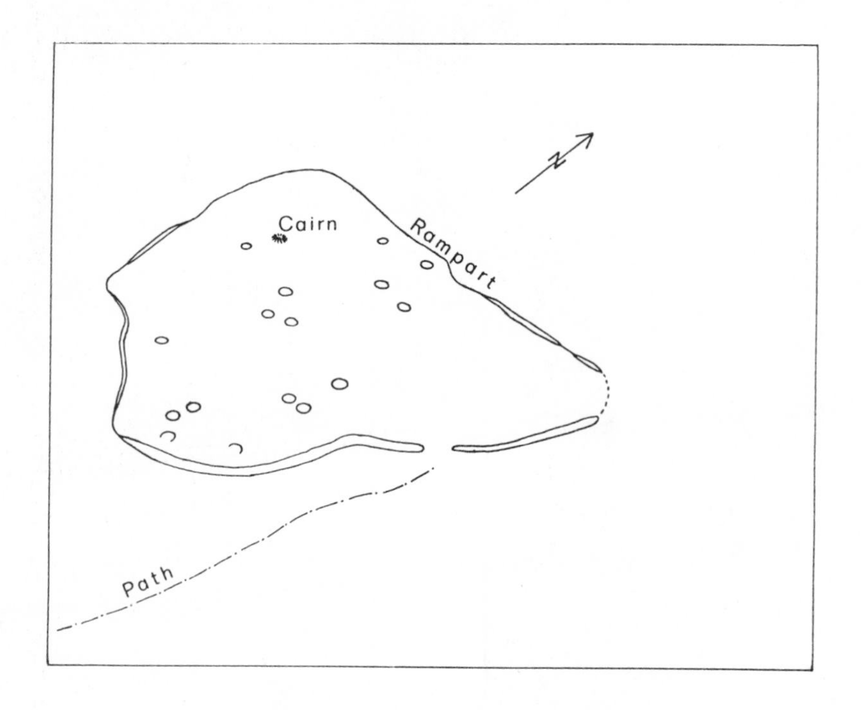

8. HILLFORT WITH HUT CIRCLES: INGLEBOROUGH NORTH YORKSHIRE

(formerly in West Riding), SD 742 746

Ingleborough is capped by a plateau of Millstone Grit, the summit of which, at 2360 ft OD (720 m), towers over the Carboniferous Limestone landscape of Craven. A rampart bank follows the edge of the plateau, except where there are vertical crags, to form a hillfort of some 15 acres (6 ha) extent. This weathered rampart is composed of gritstone blocks, laid in horizontal courses at the front and retained at the back by slabs set on edge. Many stone walled hut circles occur within the fort, their walls protruding through a thin covering of peat. More hut circles were formerly to be found, but were destroyed to build the beacon cairn and the shelter in the nineteenth century, when ground was also cleared for sports and donkey races. This destruction still goes on, and the stones of the rampart are being pulled up to build walker's cairns and shelters.

This is the highest archaeological site in the Yorkshire Pennines and it commands extensive views in all directions. No excavation has been undertaken here, and the only reported finds have been of Romano-British pottery. It has been traditional to attribute all hillforts to the Early Iron Age, but many with simple ramparts are being shown to be earlier and to belong to the Bronze Age. This high and exposed site would have been more attractive to settlement during the climatically warmer Earlier Bronze Age than in the wetter and cooler Iron Age.

T.G. Manby

Photograph by J.K. St Joseph, 25 July 1949
Cambridge University Collection.

Reference: J. Phillips, *The Rivers, Mountains and Sea Coast of Yorkshire* (London, 1853), pp. 26-29, pl. 5

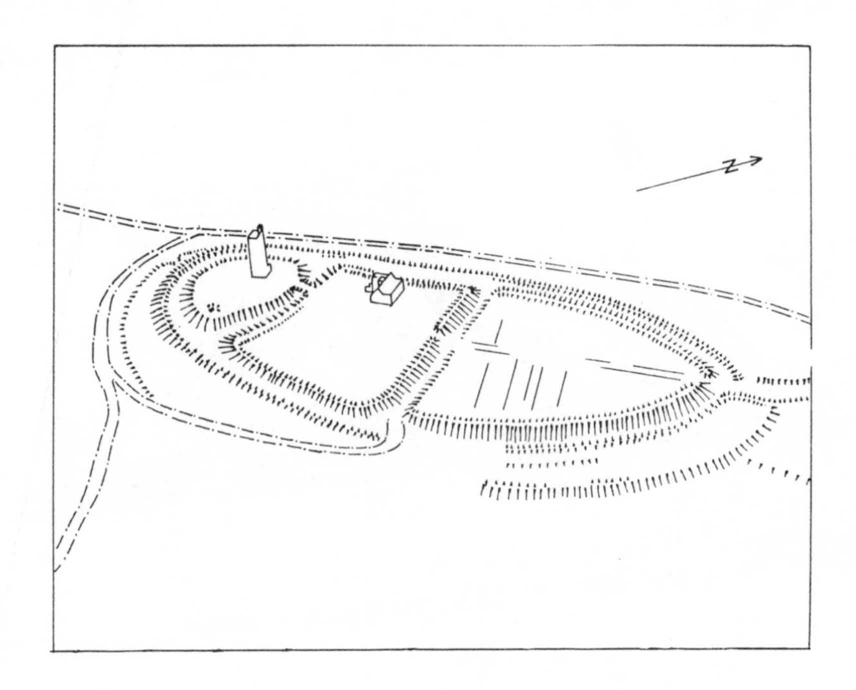

9. CASTLE HILL, ALMONDBURY, HUDDERSFIELD, WEST YORKSHIRE

(formerly in West Riding), SE 153 141

The sandstone capped outcrop of Castle Hill rises above the surrounding area of Coal Measures shales in a snowy Pennine landscape that shows up the earthworks round the summit. The hilltop was first occupied in the Late Neolithic, but in the Later Bronze Age it was developed as a hillfort. The earliest bank and ditch fortification occupied the southern (left hand) half of the hilltop. In the next phase the whole of the summit was enclosed, and further fortification later converted it into a bivallate (double rampart and ditch) hillfort. Finally, at the beginning of the Early Iron Age it was made multivallate.

The earthworks most prominently visible around the hilltop today result from the conversion of the site into a ringwork and bailey castle by the de Lacy family in the twelfth century AD. The three part medieval works consist of ringwork (left), bailey (centre, with modern hotel) and deserted town (right), in which the central street and individual property boundaries are visible. In the ringwork are the well of the castle and the tower built to commemorate the Diamond Jubilee of Queen Victoria in 1897.

T.G. Manby

Photograph by West Yorkshire Archaeology Service (R.E. Yarwood), 28 February 1977

Reference: W.J. Varley, 'A Summary of the Excavations at Castle Hill, Almondbury 1939-72', in D.W. Harding (ed.), *Hillforts: Later Prehistoric Earthworks in Britain and Ireland* (London, 1976), pp. 119-31

C
A
B
C
A
A

10. A LANDSCAPE OF FIELDS AND ENCLOSURES: GRASSINGTON, NORTH YORKSHIRE

(formerly in West Riding), SE 004 655

Light snow covers the Carboniferous Limestone landscape of Craven, and in the winter sunlight the modern field walls are seen dividing the pastures. On this land, the snow has melted on the banks of an older system of fields, so that their plan stands out. The banks are the grass grown remains of walls that originally defined small rectangular fields, between which run access lanes. In places there are enclosures with hut circles, all part of a well-developed agricultural landscape. Romano-British pottery occurs in some of the fields, showing that they were in use at that period, but the origin of the system goes back to the Bronze Age. In some instances the fields have as their nucleus a barrow or cairn, probably built during the first clearing of the woodlands that covered the ground at the time of the earliest farming colonization. The barrow in the centre of the photograph (B) was 'opened' in 1890, when an Early Bronze Age beaker was found in it, dating from about 2000 BC. Further clearing of the forest was followed by the laying out of fields for cultivation and the control of stock during the Late Bronze Age and the Early Iron Age. The local geology dictated that the fields should be enclosed by the stones that had been removed to make cultivation possible, rather than by the earthen banks and ditches used in the lowlands.

The modern field walls preserve an interesting plan. The whole area was part of the common pasture of Grassington in the Middle Ages and was not cultivated then, hence the survival of the ancient field plan. A survey of 1603 mentions the large field of irregular shape (AAA), which was an early enclosure from the common. The rest of the land was not enclosed until about 1792, and some of the fields then made were very long and narrow (CC) in order to give access to water.

T.G. Manby

Photograph by D.N. Riley, and 27 December 1980

References: A. Raistrick, 'Prehistoric Cultivations at Grassington, West Yorkshire', *Yorkshire Archaeological Journal* 33 (1936-38), pp. 166-74

S.D. Brooks, *A History of Grassington* (Clapham, 1979)

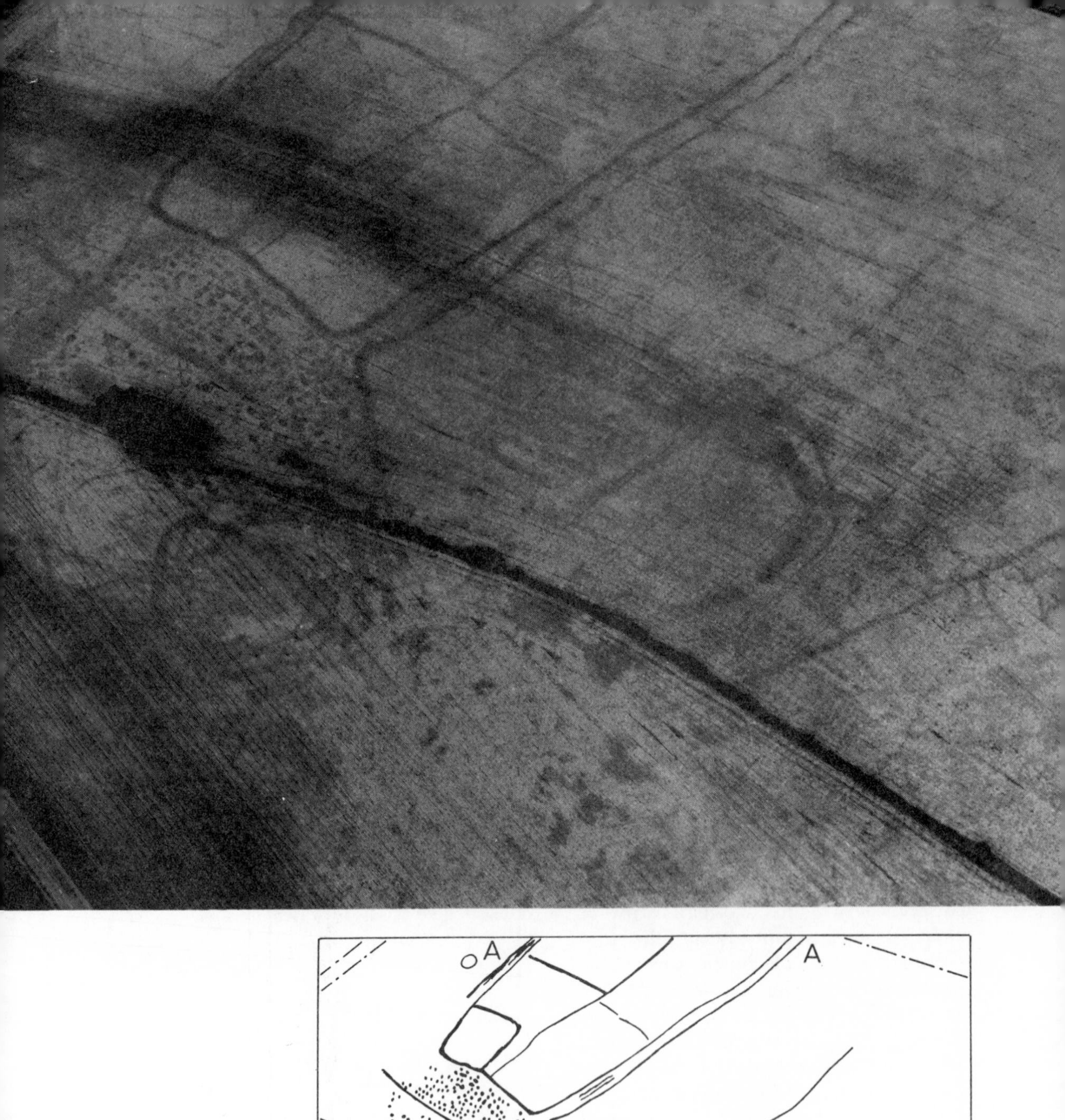

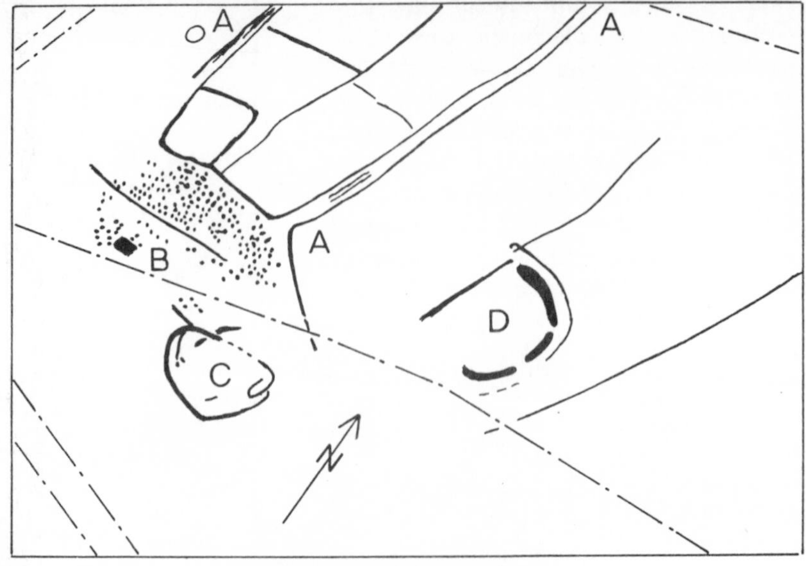
A
A
A
B
C
D

11. EARLY IRON AGE SETTLEMENT AND FIELDS: LEDSTON, WEST YORKSHIRE

(formerly in West Riding), SE 434 296

The complicated crop marks at this site on thin soil above Magnesian Limestone are due to various reasons. Areas of deeper soil cause an irregular pattern of dark patches, and a few thin lines are caused by deep cracks in the limestone. Overlying this geological pattern are prominent marks due to man-made features. Two long lanes (AA), flanked by rectangular fields, lead to a concentration of dark spots (B). Near them are marks giving the approximate plans of the ditches of an oval enclosure (C) and a D shaped enclosure with interrupted ditches (D).

Excavations in 1976 by the West Yorkshire Archaeology Unit within the cluster of dark spots confirmed the previous supposition that they indicated pits cut into the hard limestone. They had been made for storage, probably of grain, resembling similar clusters of pits found at many Iron Age settlement sites in southern England. Two pits had been reused as graves, each containing a human skeleton. There were traces of a round house and of the post holes dug for the supports of several small rectangular wooden structures, but these were too small to have produced crop marks. Finds included a small quantity of pottery and the two stones from a beehive quern. Two radiocarbon samples gave dates in the fourth and second centuries BC.

T.G. Manby

Photograph by D.N. Riley, 10 July 1976

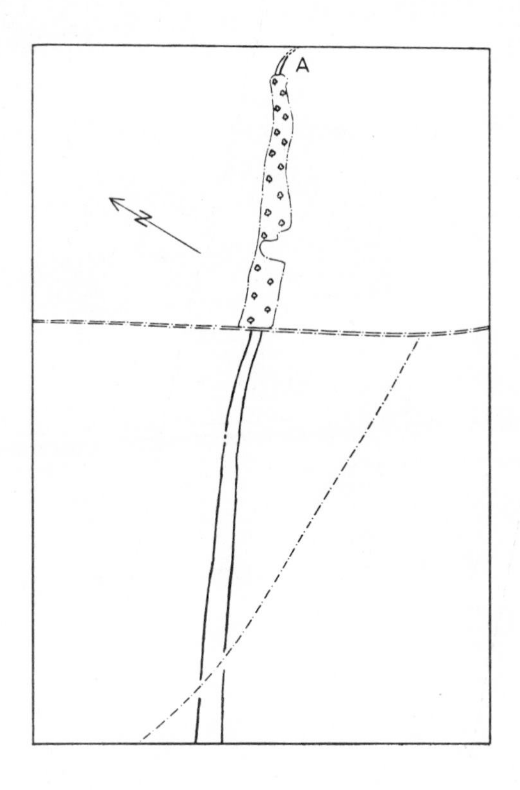

12. LINEAR EARTHWORK: WEAVERTHORPE, NORTH YORKSHIRE

(formerly in East Riding), SE 973 678

Part of the Great Wold Dyke is here seen as a crop mark in the cornfields. The left-hand (northern) mark is a continuous line, caused by the filling of a deep ditch. The right-hand (southern) mark is a broken line, perhaps caused by pits dug in the base of a ditch, but more probably by an effect of cultivation, since the line is continuous on photographs taken in other years. In the long plantation the earthwork has been preserved and consists of a bank with a ditch hollow on the northern side. In the distance, beyond the plantation, two parallel crop marks can be seen again (A). This is one part of a dyke that can be traced continuously for twelve miles, with many branches joining it; part of an extensive system of earthworks dividing the Wolds into territorial blocks. The earliest of these linear earthworks were constructed in the Late Bronze Age and the system was added to in the Early Iron Age and later periods, when their functions possibly changed. Many miles of dykes have been destroyed since the Middle Ages, but isolated lengths often survive as earthworks to the present day, still used as boundaries for parishes, farms and fields.

T.G. Manby

Photograph by D.N. Riley, 30 July 1981

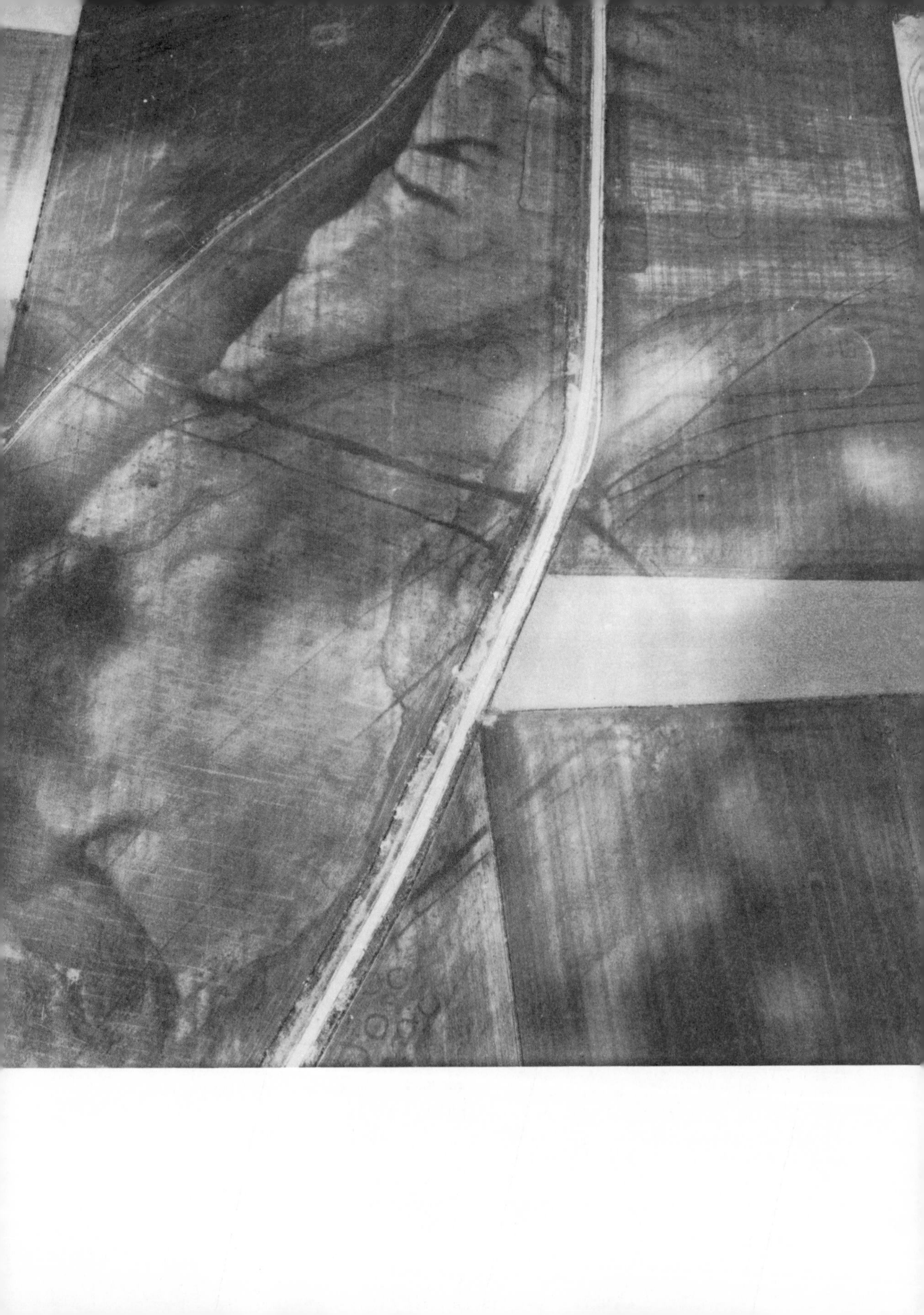

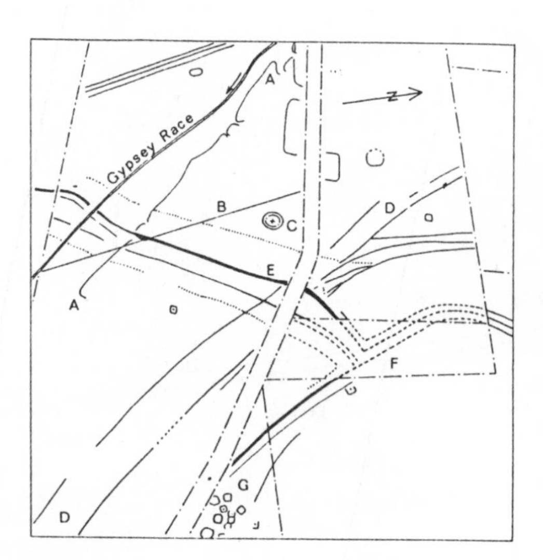

13. MULTI-PERIOD LANDSCAPE: BURTON FLEMING, NORTH HUMBERSIDE

(formerly in East Riding), TA 074 724

This illustration of the crops growing on the gravel floor of the Great Wold Valley gives a wide diversity of information. The first point to notice is the geological division between thin soil with paler toned crops to the right of line AA on the drawing and, to the left, alluvial soil with darker toned crops near the Gypsey Race stream. There is also unevenness of tone because of cloud shadows. On this background are dark crop marks on buried archaeological features.

The two parallel lines DD may perhaps mark the ditches of a Neolithic cursus (compare 2), though this interpretation is not certain. Other dark lines indicate field boundaries, probably of Iron Age date. The most important are the double and triple lines indicating the former ditches of bank and ditch earthworks. Another type of boundary is marked by lines of pits, or possibly post holes, appearing as lines of dark spots, two of which run across the centre of the photograph parallel to a big boundary ditch E (compare 12). The crop mark of this ditch disappears in a small pale toned field F, but its continuation has been shown on the drawing by broken lines. It is known from photographs taken in other years that it makes a T junction in this field with another big ditch FG.

Also dating from the Iron Age are burials surrounded by square ditches (compare 15). The largest group of about 20 is at the base of the photograph (G), and other isolated burals are seen faintly in the centre.

A medieval feature is the site of a windmill mound (C). The cross foundation trenches for the base of the wooden mill tower make a distinct mark, as does the circular trench that surrounded the mound. The enclosure of the former open fields is 1769 was responsible for the big modern fields with their straight hedge lines and the road with its broad grass margins. The dark line B shows where one of these straight hedges has been removed recently.

T.G. Manby and L.A.S. Butler

Photograph by A.L. Pacitto

References: Royal Commission on Historical Monuments (England), *A Matter of Time* (1961), pp. 28-31, pl. 11

Victoria County History of Yorkshire: the East Riding, vol. II (1974), pp. 119-25

14. BARROWS AND PIT ALIGNMENTS: THREE HOWES RIGG, DANBY, NORTH YORKSHIRE

(formerly in North Riding), NZ 740 107

This moorland photograph shows, reading from top to bottom, a line of three large Bronze Age round barrows or cairns (the Three Howes), two bomb craters of the Second World War and a double line of pits. The pale tone of two of the Howes is due to a growth of bracken, which contrasts with the surrounding heather. All three barrows had been subjected to 'merciless and repeated disturbance' before the excavation of the central mound by Canon Atkinson in 1856. Here he found sherds of a large broken cinerary urn and an accessory cup, with calcined human bones and flints, and a second accessory cup, all in the south eastern part of the mound. They date the Howe to the Earlier Bronze Age.

The double pit alignment is the celebrated 'British village' of the Victorian antiquaries, the scene of many excursions in the period when such pits were thought to have been dwellings. No evidence of settlement has ever been found in them, and they are now generally accepted as boundary markers, similar in purpose to linear earthworks (12). Pit alignments shown by crop marks are common in some parts of England, including the Wolds (e.g. 13), but, except in a few remote places such as Three Howes Rigg, all have been levelled by agriculture.

D.A. Spratt

Photograph by North Yorkshire County Council Planning Department (P. Chadwick), 30 January 1980

References: Canon J.C. Atkinson, *Gentlemen's Magazine*, 1865, pt 1, pp. 16-19
F. Elgee, *Early Man in North-East Yorkshire* (Gloucester, 1932), pp. 150-52

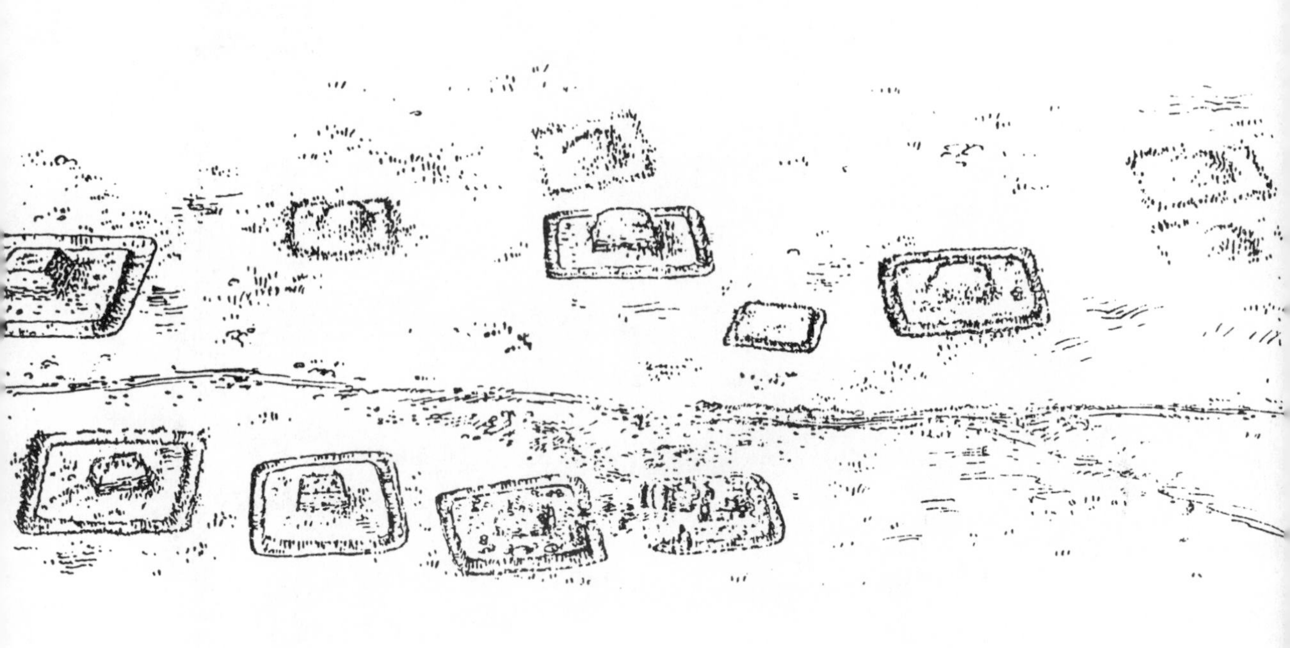

15. SQUARE DITCHED BARROWS OF THE EARLY IRON AGE UNDER EXCAVATION: RUDSTON, NORTH HUMBERSIDE
(formerly in East Riding), TA 093 703

Removal of the surface soil during the excavation of part of an extensive cemetery on the floor of the Great Wold Valley north of Rudston has produced soil marks that give the positions of a number of square barrows, the original appearance of which is suggested by the drawing. They were first recorded as a spread of square crop marks, caused by the deep soil fillings of the barrow ditches dug into the chalk gravel subsoil. At the centre of the space enclosed by each ditch is a grave containing an inhumation burial. Gravel dug from the ditches was originally heaped over the graves to form low mounds. The ditches later became filled with soil by natural weathering processes. During the Middle Ages the mounds marking the graves were levelled by ploughing, which has continued until the present day. The parallel strips of soil crossing the excavated area are the deeper furrows dividing the strips of medieval rigg and furrow cultivation (compare 26, 32 and 35).

T.G. Manby

Photograph by D.N. Riley, 10 July 1972
Reference: I.M. Stead, 'La Tène Burials between Burton Fleming and Rudston, North Humberside', *Antiquaries Journal* 56 (1976), pp. 217-26

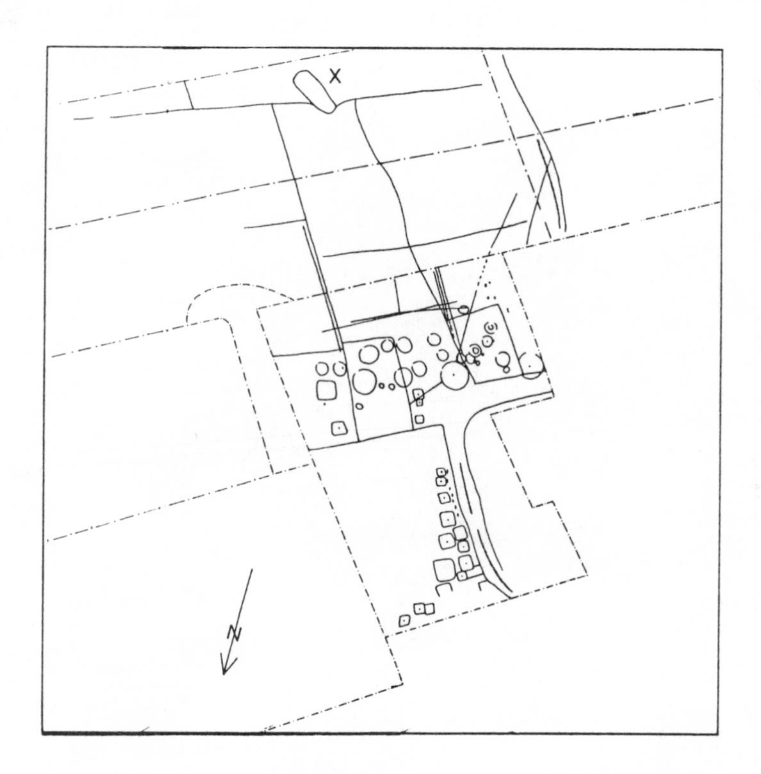

16. RING DITCHES, SQUARE BARROWS AND ENCLOSURES: RILLINGTON, NORTH YORKSHIRE
(formerly in East Riding), SE 856 744

A group of unusually clear crop marks on land with chalk gravel subsoil is situated in an area that has partly been engulfed by modern housing. There is a central group of circular marks of the type known as ring ditches, the largest of which has a diagonal ditch running away from it. Some of the rings have entrance gaps on their southern (more distant) side, suggesting that they may have been ring foundation trenches for houses. Below is a cemetery of square ditched barrows of Iron Age type, in some of which the central graves are apparent (compare 15). Beside them are the two ditches which bounded the track of a field lane, associated with a pattern of rectilinear field boundaries. One ring ditch clearly pre-dates the field boundary cutting across it. The elongated lighter mark (X) at the top of the photograph is respected by the field ditches diverted round it, and may be the site of a long barrow, a type of burial mound of Neolithic date. Trial excavation of the field ditches produced pottery of Early Iron Age date. Evidence of Anglian burials also comes from this site, and it may be noted that ring ditches and square ditched features occur at some Anglo-Saxon cemeteries in Eastern England.

T.G. Manby

Photograph by A.L. Pacitto

Reference: P. Turnbull, 'Excavations at Rillington, 1980', *Yorkshire Archaeological Journal* 55 (1983), pp. 1-9

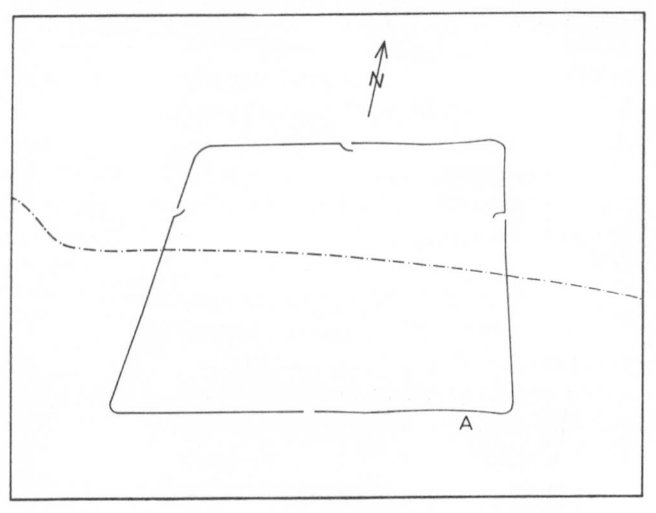
A

17. ROMAN TEMPORARY CAMP, MALHAM: NORTH YORKSHIRE

(formerly West Riding), SE 915 655

Vegetius, a Roman military writer, said that the Roman army carried a walled town with them wherever they marched. He was referring to their capability of defending with rampart and ditch their leather-tented camp at each overnight stopping place whilst on campaign in hostile territory. The well preserved rampart and incomplete ditch of such a marching camp, a square of 20 acres (8.2 ha), large enough to hold the six thousand men of a legion, are clearly visible on this photograph, which was taken with the low sunlight of a summer evening. Note how at three of the entrances there are traces of a semi-circular inturn (usually known by the Latin name of *clavicula*) to strengthen the defences, though they are shown more clearly on the drawing than by this photograph. Such *claviculae* are usually an indication of a first-century date. The rough wet ground extending well into the eastern (right) side of the camp was in the same state in Roman times; this is the cause of the slight bend in the south rampart at A. The site was probably chosen in a dry summer.

Mastiles Lane, which can be seen crossing the site centrally from west to east, is itself of some age, and several earlier lines of the lane can be seen crossing the western (left) rampart, fanning out to find the best crossing of the small ravine.

H.G. Ramm

Photograph by D.N. Riley, 21 June 1977
Reference: J.K. St Joseph, 'Air Reconnaissance in Britain 1955-57', *Journal of Roman Studies* 48 (1958), pp. 86-101 (see p. 97)

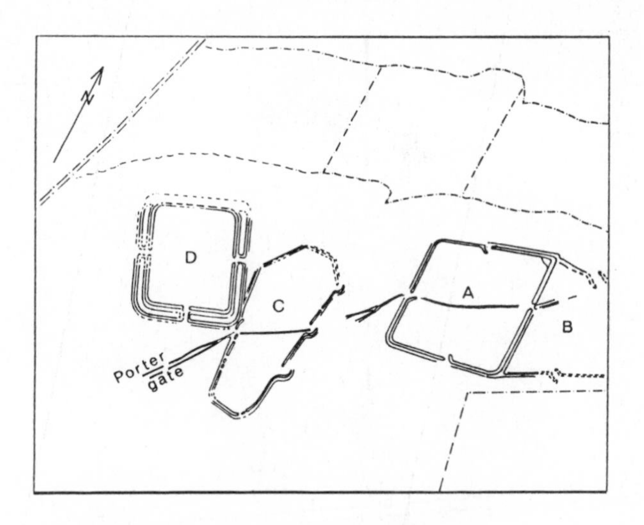

18. ROMAN FORTS AND CONSTRUCTION CAMPS: CAWTHORN, NORTH YORKSHIRE

(formerly in North Riding), SE 783 900

There are four sets of Roman defences on this site, remaining as standing earthworks, but obscured in places by trees and bushes: two forts (A and D) and two temporary camps (B and C). On the left are the double ditches and turf rampart of fort D, 3.5 acres (1.5 ha) in area, which could have accommodated a standard Roman army infantry cohort of five hundred men. Two gates are visible and there is a west gate hidden by trees, but there was never a north gate, since it would have opened on to the edge of a steep slope. One corner of its outer ditch destroyed part of the ditch and bank of the earlier coffin shaped camp C, which has three gates, all on the west side and defended by external *claviculae*. This was the defended camp of soldiers temporarily occupying the site whilst working on the construction of fort A, for which purpose the gates were convenient. A is a larger fort than D 6.6 acres (2.6 ha) in area, with a simpler ditch system. This fort was never finished. Later its east side was slighted and its other defences were continued eastwards to form the extension B. Both A and B then formed a large construction camp, made to house the troops building D. Part of B is visible, but its eastern half is off the photograph. The relationship of the works to one another and their general date (AD 80–120) was established in excavations by Sir Ian Richmond in 1923–29; he argued that they were the work of legionaries from York who twice used this waterless plateau for exercises in fort building. Nowadays more favourable consideration is given to the possibility that D, at least, was intended for permanent occupation.

A medieval and later road, the Portergate runs across the site. The dark band on the photograph running from the south gate of D, across C and to the inside of A, to turn south is a filled in trench bulldozed as a firebreak to contain a moor fire. The site is owned by the North York Moors National Park and is open to the public.

H.G. Ramm

Photograph by D.R. Wilson, 31 May 1968

Reference: I.A. Richmond, 'The Four Roman Camps at Cawthorn in the North Riding of Yorkshire', *Archaeological Journal* 89 (1932), pp. 17-78

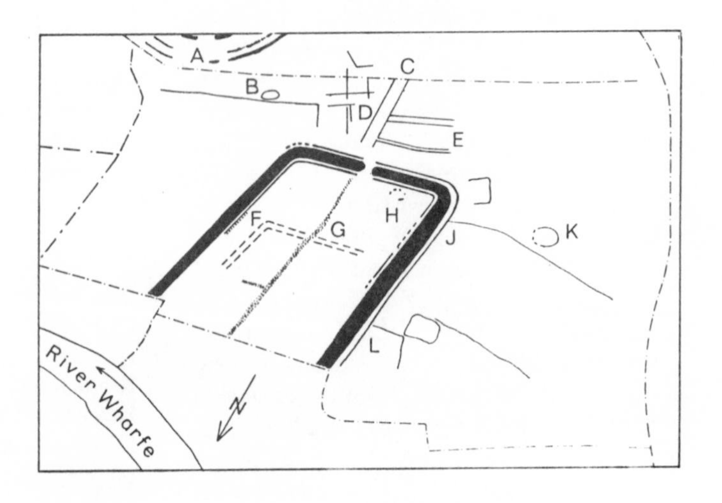
A
B
C
D
E
F
G
H
J
K
L
River Wharfe

19. ROMAN FORT: NEWTON KYME, NORTH YORKSHIRE

(formerly in West Riding), SE 456 454

The 'playing card' shape of a Roman fort is clearly visible in the centre of the photograph, typically sited at the river crossing of a major Roman road. The plan of the defences is given by crop marks, a wide dark band with narrow inner and outer lines. Excavations in 1956/57 found that the outer line marked the outer ditch of a system of three ditches, the two inner of which had been later converted to a single wide ditch, the cause of the wide dark band. The inner line shows the former position of a 3 m wide wall of heavy rubble; where this line is dark it probably runs over a foundation trench from which the wall has been almost completely removed by stone robbers, though at F a thin white line (stippled on the drawing) shows where a little of the wall may remain below the ground. This defensive system gives the outline of an earlier and a later fort, which were both of the same size (about 4 hectares or 10 acres). Within the ditches was the base of a rampart, which was overlain by the remains of occupation of civilian type dating from the early second century. Another air photograph, published by Professor St Joseph, shows the double ditches (marked on the plan by broken lines) of two sides of a third fort, smaller in size, the northern and western defences of which coincide with those of the other forts. The light toned crop mark running through the centre of the defences is the line of a road; it bends slightly at G, where it crosses the ditches of the small fort. The sequence of events represented by these remains was (a) in the first century AD, the construction of a small fort for a cohort of 500 men, which was later replaced by a large fort for a cavalry regiment of 1000 men, (b) from the early second century, a civil occupation, and (c) at the turn of the third and fourth centuries, the reinstatement of the large fort.

Beyond the fort, crop marks show the boundary ditches of the plots in a Roman civil settlement or *vicus*, through which runs a road, defined by marks on its side ditches (C). A short branch road (E) leaves it. At D the plot boundaries run at an oblique angle to the road C and to the axis of the forts; on the same alignment within the fort at H, extending below the defences, the excavations found evidence of timber buildings of Roman military type, which must have been earlier than the road and all known forts.

There is more on the photograph. The curved crop marks (A) at the top show part of a large Neolithic henge; the ring ditch B is probably the site of Bronze Age round barrow; near H may be seen the marks on some of a circle of large pits surrounding a Bronze Age burial with a food-vessel; another ring ditch shows faintly at K. The fort defences intersect older ditches at J and L.

H.G. Ramm

Photograph by D.N. Riley, 23 July 1979

Reference: S.S. Frere, and J.K. St Joseph, *Roman Britain from the Air* (Cambridge, 1983), pp. 110-13

Postscript: In *Britannia* XVIII (1987), p. 12, G.S. Maxwell and D.R. Wilson have put forward an alternative explanation for the small internal enclosure.

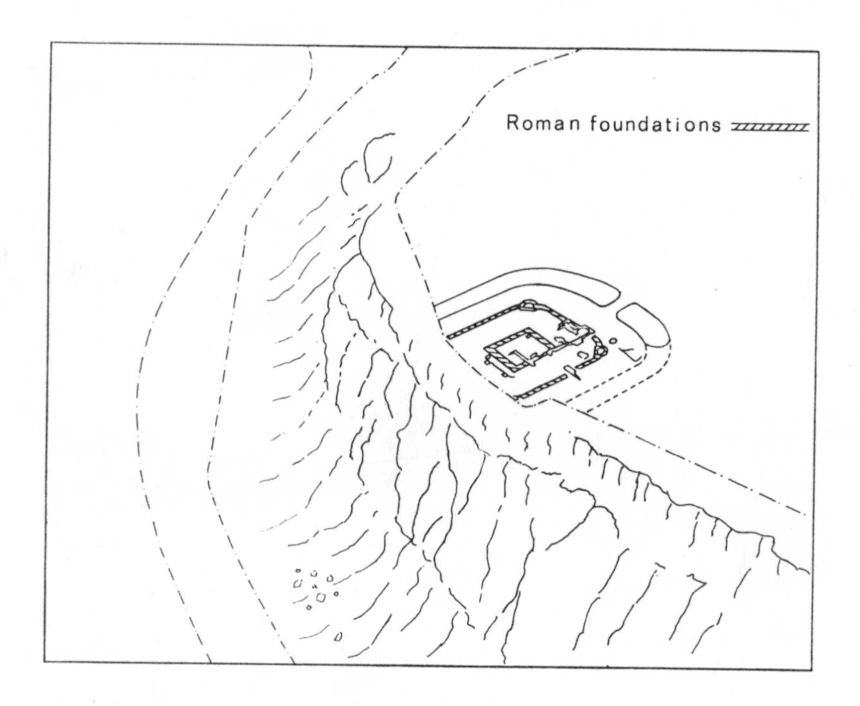

20. ROMAN SIGNAL TOWER: SCARBOROUGH, NORTH YORKSHIRE

(formerly North Riding), TA 052 891

This tower stood in a dramatic position on the lip of a steep cliff promontory overlooking the sea. An inscription describes the similar earthwork at Ravenscar as *turrem et castrum*, tower and fort, a very exact description. The platform of the fort, square with rounded corners, is defined by a ditch, two sides of which have been excavated and stabilized, a third still filled is just visible and the fourth has been eroded with the cliff and lost. Set back on the platform are the foundations of a defensive wall with small projecting turrets at the angles. Inside this are the square foundations of a tower which rose high above the cliff to provide a clear view out to sea. From it watchers could keep lookout for raiders and coordinate the activities of patrolling ships, relaying signals from ship to ship and along a line of coastal towers that extended from Filey to Saltburn and perhaps beyond in both directions. These towers date from the reconstruction of Britain's defences after the catastrophes of AD 367.

The pieces of later walling cutting across the Roman foundations belong to the Norman chapel of Our Lady, as altered in the fourteenth century. The chapel had a pre-conquest origin, but was rebuilt with the Norman castle, in the precincts of which it stood. The small round structure by the Roman north-west turret is the Norman well of Our Lady.

H.G. Ramm

Photograph by North Yorkshire County Council Planning Department (P. Chadwick), 13 March 1980

Reference: A. Rowntree (ed.), *History of Scarborough* (London, 1931), pp. 40-50, 146-48

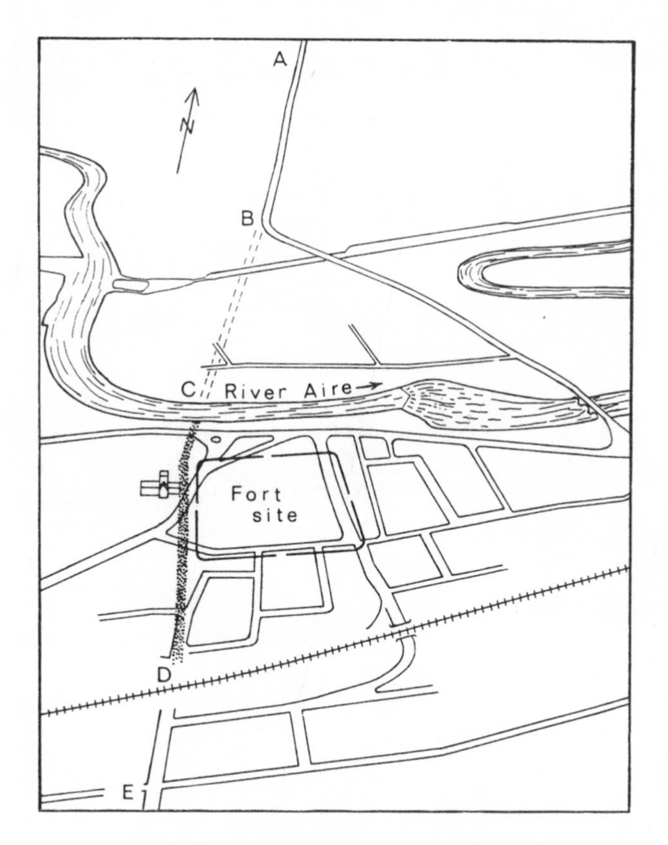

21. ROMAN ROAD: CASTLEFORD, WEST YORKSHIRE

(formerly in West Riding), SE 426 260

In the background of the picture the straight course of the modern A656 follows the line of the Roman road to York, illustrating the ruthless directness of the Roman surveyor. The continuation of the road can only be presumed from B to C, but its line has been fairly well established between C and D, where excavations have revealed it at several points. In the left foreground the modern street south of the railway (E) represents the Roman road to Doncaster. There was probably a wooden bridge at C, where the road crossed the river Aire. The crossing was defended by a fort built in the first century AD and abandoned in the second. The site is now covered by streets and houses, but parts have been excavated in recent years. The drawing shows the approximate outline of its defences, east of the recent parish church. South of the fort, extending at least to the railway, was the *vicus* or civilian settlement.

Any Roman bridge had disappeared by the tenth century, when Castleford was called 'at Ceasterforde', the ford by the Roman fort. A grid of Victorian streets and modern developments have obscured the lines of the older town centred round the church and along the road from it to the Aire bridge, first mentioned in 1507. The movement of the main road and river crossing downstream is due to the attraction of Pontefract as a destination.

H.G. Ramm

Photograph by West Yorkshire Archaeological Service (R.E. Yarwood), 15 June 1983

References: I.D. Margary, *Roman Roads in Britain* (3rd edn, London, 1973), p. 415

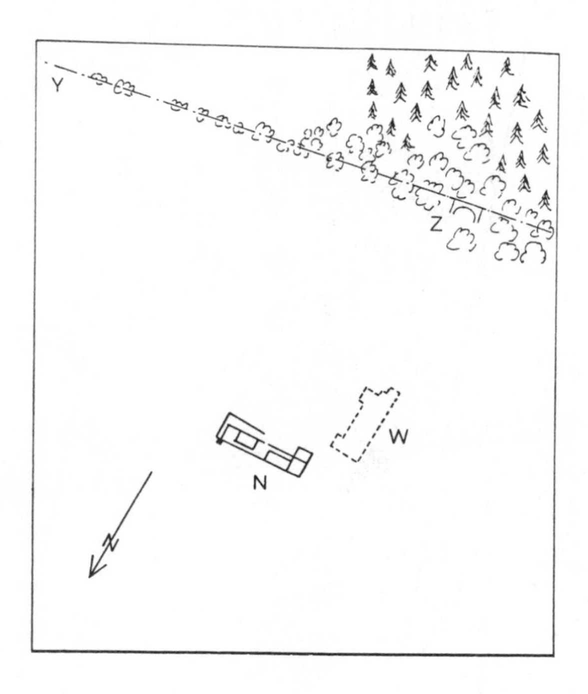

22. ROMAN VILLA UNDER EXCAVATION: BEADLAM, NORTH YORKSHIRE

(formerly in North Riding), SE 634 841

The well-preserved remains of a Roman country house, which had long survived as grass covered mounds, were recognized as Roman when the field was ploughed for the first time in 1964. A brief trial excavation in 1966 was followed by a full-scale excavation in the summer of 1969. The buildings were grouped on three sides of a courtyard with its open end facing south. Only the north and west sides were excavated, and when this photograph was taken only the north building (N) had been uncovered. This building was one of the residential parts of the villa; one room was floored by a mosaic pavement of geometric design, some of the rooms had been heated and there were traces of a staircase to an upper floor. The west building (W), which proved to be a typical example of the type of Roman building known as a corridor house, had an attached bath house. The excavations were intended to uncover the site for future display, and therefore only the latest fourth century AD buildings on the site were revealed. The farm buildings normally associated with this type of house have still to be found.

At the top right of the photograph the River Riccal is crossed by the remains of a bridge which was originally part of the old Helmsley-Pickering railway line (YZ).

H.G. Ramm

Photograph by A.L. Pacitto, Summer 1969
Reference: I.M. Stead, 'Beadlam Roman Villa: an Interim Report', *Yorkshire Archaeological Journal* 43 (1971), pp. 178-86

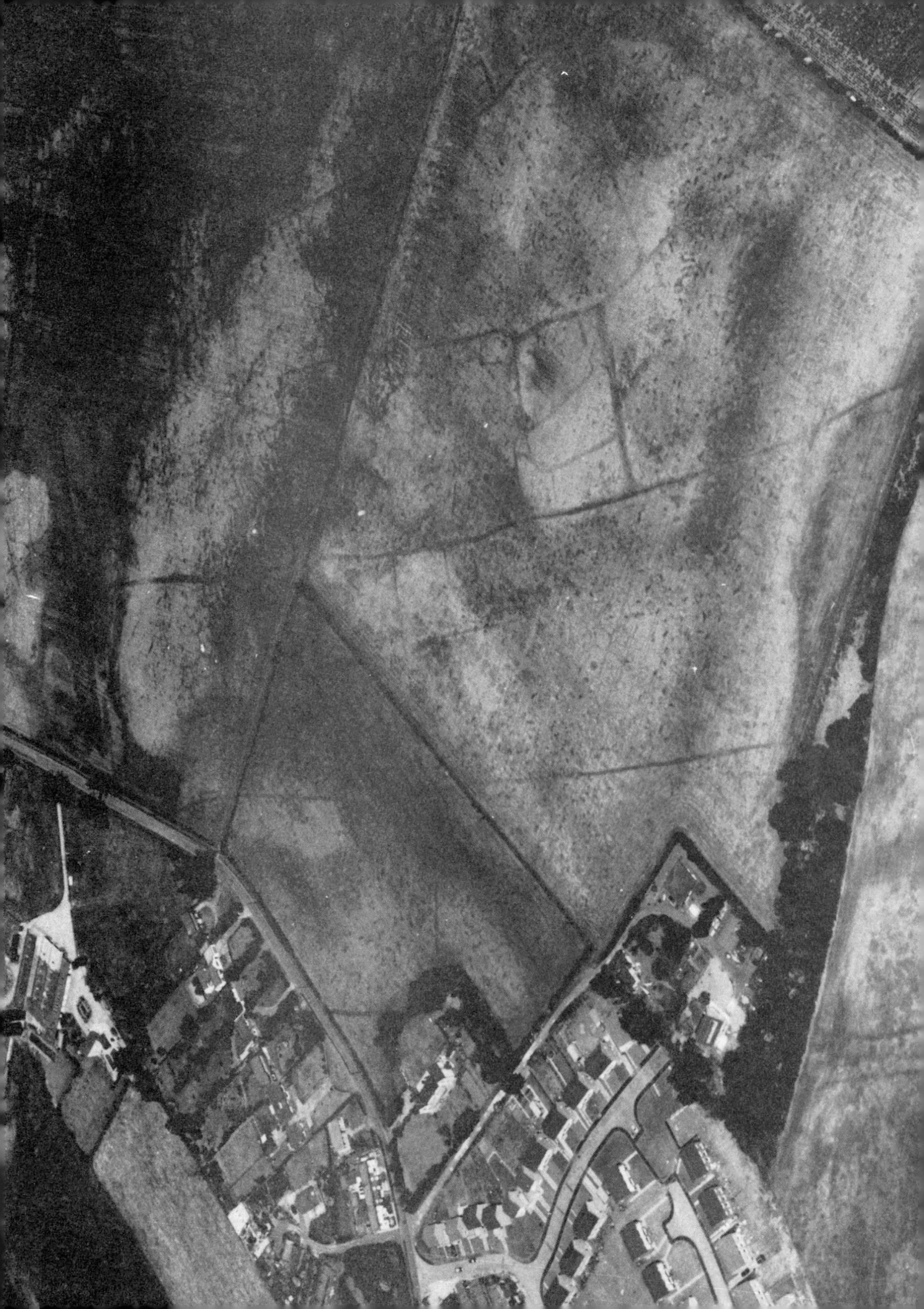

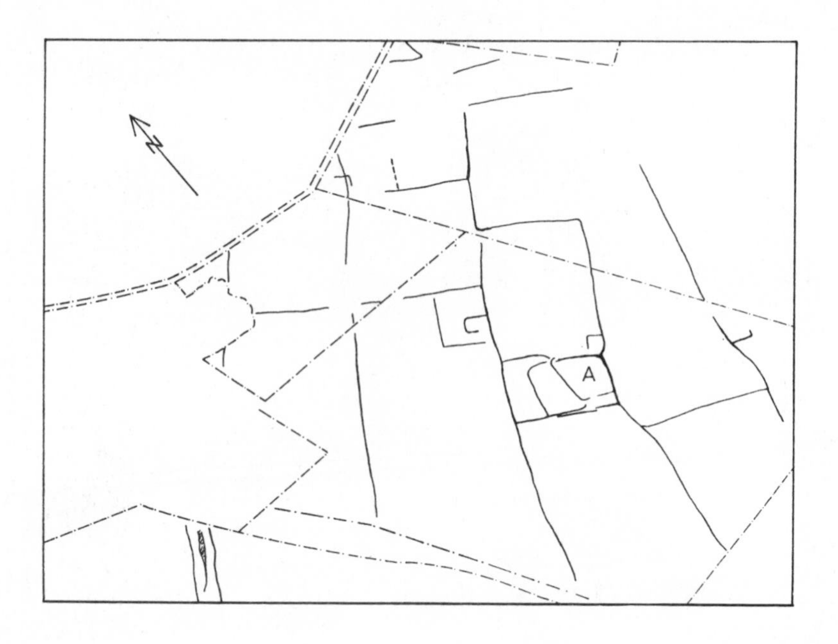

23. ANCIENT FIELDS: LITTLEWORTH, ROSSINGTON, SOUTH YORKSHIRE

(formerly in West Riding), SK 632 981

In the fields near the houses of Littleworth are seen several parallel dark lines of crop marks, which have no relation to the present-day land boundaries. These long lines and the short lines at right angles connecting them show a system of ditches, now filled in, that must have been made as boundaries of a planned layout of fields older than the modern fields and roads. Several small enclosures (A) probably give the site of a farmstead or of pens for stock. Similar crop marks of the boundaries of early fields occur often on a belt of light soils above the Bunter Sandstone extending from the Doncaster area southwards into Nottinghamshire. They cover perhaps 10,000 acres (4000 ha) of land in total, and no doubt stretched over much more land on which crop marks do not appear. Their date has not yet been firmly established, but excavations at sites in Nottinghamshire have found that enclosures connected with similar field boundaries were being used in the second and third centuries AD. Some areas of fields of this type may have been laid out before the Roman period, but this is a matter of speculation.

D.N. Riley

Photograph by D.N. Riley, 29 June 1975
Reference: D.N. Riley, *Early Landscape from the Air* (Sheffield, 1980), p. 12

24. DANES DYKE, FLAMBOROUGH HEAD, NORTH HUMBERSIDE

(formerly in East Riding), TA 216 694—213 732.

Looking south across Flamborough Head, this view shows the whole length of the massive earthwork known as Danes Dyke, which runs for about 2½ miles (4 km) to cut off about 5 square miles (13 sq km) of headland on the left side (the east) of the photograph. The bank and ditch show well in the foreground, beyond which the earthworks are hidden by a line of woods. Their present height is about 26 ft (8 m) from the top of the bank to the bottom of the ditch. There were two entrances through the Dyke, one of which has been damaged by the modern road. The ditch is on the right side on the photograph (the west).

The Danes Dyke differs in scale and constructional details from the Yorkshire Wolds boundary dykes (12), with which it has often been associated. It probably also differed in function, and can only be described as a fortification. There is little information about its date. The evidence obtained during excavations made many years ago by General Pitt-Rivers suggests that the bank was made in the Bronze Age or later, but gives no precise information. If it were an Iron Age construction, the Dyke could be interpreted as the western fortification of an *oppidum*, or major defended area, protected on the other side by the sea cliffs, like those in the foreground. It would be comparable to, though more extensive that the area protected by the Iron Age defences at Stanwick (26). An alternative explanation is a fortified beach head of the Dark Age, made by an invading force landing at one or both of the two small coves that breach the cliffs. In this case the Dyke might have been built in the sixth century AD after the arrival at Flamborough of Ida with a fleet of sixty ships, but before he moved north to Bamburgh.

H.G. Ramm

Photograph by D.N. Riley, 14 March 1985
Reference: H.G. Ramm, 'Danes Dyke, Flamborough', *Archaeological Journal* 141 (1984), pp. 37-39

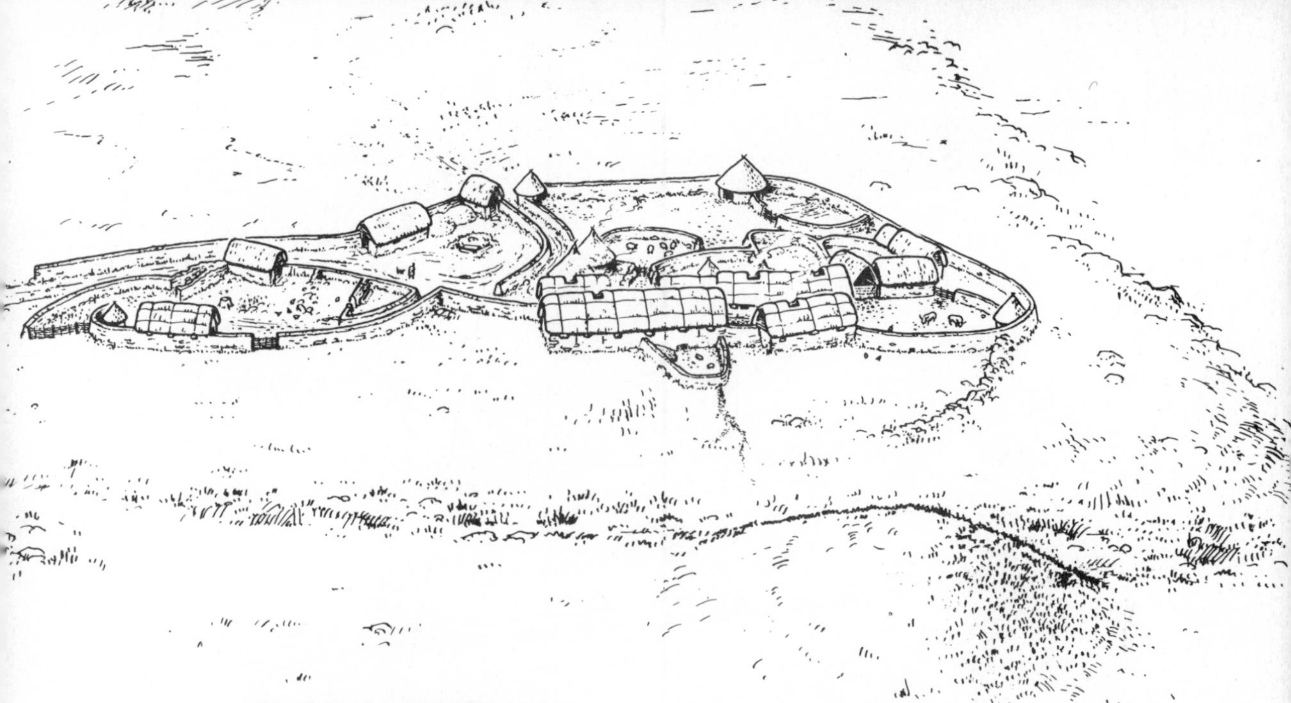

25. SETTLEMENT SITE: LEA GREEN, GRASSINGTON, NORTH YORKSHIRE

(formerly West Riding), SD 996 663

The light of the evening sun throws into relief the ruins of an ancient settlement on the exposed limestone pavement one mile (2 km) north-west of Grassington, not far from the area shown before (10). There are three features of particular interest in the vicinity. The first is the remains of a barrow or large cairn (lower right) which stands on a natural hillock; the stones have been used to build the field walls near it, but the circular base is obvious. This cairn was excavated in 1893 and was found to contain seven burials, for which a Late Bronze Age or Early Iron Age date has been suggested.

The second main feature is the ruined settlement consisting of rectangular buildings and sub-rectangular yards (centre), now represented by low stone walls. The drawing suggests its original appearance. Most of the structures lie within an enclosing wall, but there are some other buildings (centre left) outside this. The settlement was excavated in 1893 by Professor Boyd Dawkins, who considered that the farm had been in use from the late Early Iron Age until the third century AD. However, although the finds are of this date, the possibility that the site continued in Celtic occupation until the Viking invasions cannot be ruled out, particularly on the evidence of similar continuity in North Welsh hut groups.

The third feature needing comment is the line of craters, marking old lead-mining pits (compare 41), which follow a seam of ore (top right, running diagonally). Low banks in the same area show the positions of early field walls, which follow curving lines, in contrast to the straight eighteenth- or nineteenth-century walls still in use or recently abandoned. A dew pond (lower left) is a dark circle.

L.A.S. Butler

Photograph by D.N. Riley, 26 May 1977

References: H. Speight, *Proceedings of the Yorkshire Geological Society* 12 (1894), pp. 378-81

A. Raistrick, 'Prehistoric Cultivations at Grassington', *Yorkshire Archaeological Journal* 33 (1936-38), pp. 166-74

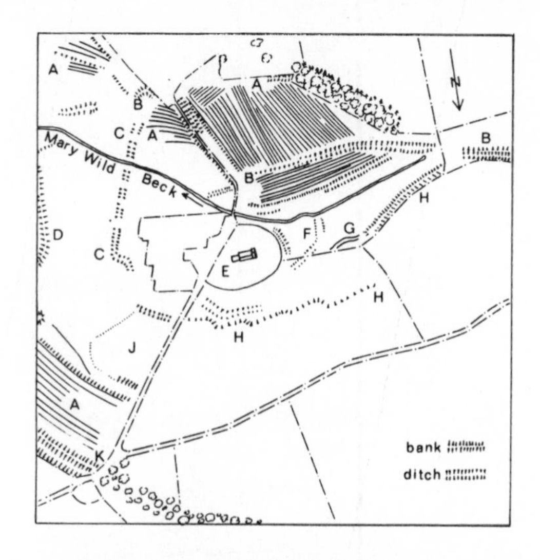

26. ST. JOHN'S CHURCH, STANWICK, NORTH YORKSHIRE

(formerly in North Riding), NZ 185 120

The church of St John (E) stands in the midst of a vast complex of Iron Age earthworks that enclose about 850 acres. Lengths of these earthworks appear at K in the foreground, at D on the left edge and at BBB beyond the Mary Wild Beck, which wanders across the field of view. The present course of the beck is relatively modern; other water-courses are also visible (F and G), together with some transverse drainage channels. The churchyard with its curvilinear boundary is the focus of the picture. It is of a kind that is called 'early'—a euphemism for the seventh or eighth century—by analogy with Christian sites of comparable form in Ireland. Unfortunately, the Irish sites are for the most part as imprecisely dated and little understood as their English counterparts. Here, all that can be argued from the landscape is that the curvilinear churchyard enclosure existed before the modern road that has truncated its eastern side. An arc of the former surround, consisting of an inner ditch and outer bank, is still to be seen due west of the church. The bank shows well, reflecting the sun which is shining from the west.

A monastic layout of 'Irish' type at Stanwick is not out of the question. A monastery of Hiberno-Northumbrian character was established nearby at Gilling in the seventh century. Gilling, like Stanwick, has a curvilinear churchyard. Moreover, there are historical reasons for believing that the two sites were once associated: perhaps, like Wearmouth/Jarrow, or Columbanus' communities in the Vosges, there was 'one monastery in several places'.

Many other low earthworks remind us of the history of this place. At AAA is the rigg and furrow of medieval strip cultivation, and the zig-zag banks HHH mark the ends of further medieval strips which have been levelled by modern cultivation of the land to the north. There are medieval manorial earthworks at J. The modern road is a replacement for an older road, seen at CC in the large field to the left of the modern road. The remaining banks and ditches in this field are related to post-medieval activities. This is a remarkable photograph, packed with incident, and to be valued as much for its record of the medieval and earlier landscape as for the ecclesiastical centrepiece.

R.K. Morris and H.G. Ramm

Photograph by A.L. Pacitto

Reference: the churchyard earthworks have not been published previously but the Iron Age remains are described by Sir Mortimer Wheeler, *The Stanwick Fortifications* (London, 1954)

27. ALL SAINTS' CHURCH, BRAMHAM, WEST YORKSHIRE

(formerly in West Riding), SE 428 431

The air photograph of Bramham church emphasizes the unusual character of the site and immediately raises the question whether this was a religious community in the pre-Viking period. Three factors are suggestive. Firstly, Bramham, like Stanwick, is close to the line of a Roman road (off, left margin). Good communications were important to the founders of religious communities. Secondly, the churchyard is large and is oval in shape, greater than the needs of the present village burials; but of course many churchyards have at least one curved side, often where a passing road has influenced the shape. Thirdly, and most significantly, the church stands on the western edge of the churchyard. In the period 650–850 religious communities often possessed several churches in a single enclosure. In Ireland it was not unusual for an oratory to adhere to the boundary. Despite the absence of documentary record, it is this combination of factors which marks out Bramham as a candidate for future study.

R.K. Morris

Photograph by West Yorkshire Archaeology Service (R.E. Yarwood), May 1985

28. EARLY NORMAN CHURCH AND RINGWORK: KIPPAX, WEST YORKSHIRE

(formerly West Riding), SE 417 304

An alternative form of Norman castle is the ringwork and bailey (compare 9). This photograph shows the early Norman church of Kippax and near it the eastern ringwork of Manor Garth Hill (lower right). The bailey lies beneath the cemetery (lower left). Kippax was the head of a large estate which belonged to Earl Edwin in 1066, but by the mid twelfth century was in the hands of the powerful Lacy family. In the reorganization of the extensive honour of Pontefract, of which Kippax now formed part, the northern administrative centre was established at Barwick in Elmet. Here, only four miles (6 km) from Kippax, a substantial motte was constructed within a massive earlier earthwork of probable prehistoric origin. The reduction in status of Kippax probably explains the simplicity of the Manor Garth Hill ringwork, the plan of which and the absence of stone defences (the stone structure on the bank is a modern seat) suggest that it is a rare undisturbed survival of a late Saxon or early Norman defended site.

The photograph does not reflect the prominent hill-top position of the site, with its commanding view southwards over Calder valley.

S.A. Moorhouse

Photograph by West Yorkshire Archaeology Service (R.E. Yarwood), 8 September 1978
Reference: M.L. Faull, and S. Moorhouse (eds.), *West Yorkshire: An Archaeological Survey to AD 1500* (Wakefield, 1981), p. 735 and pl. 8A

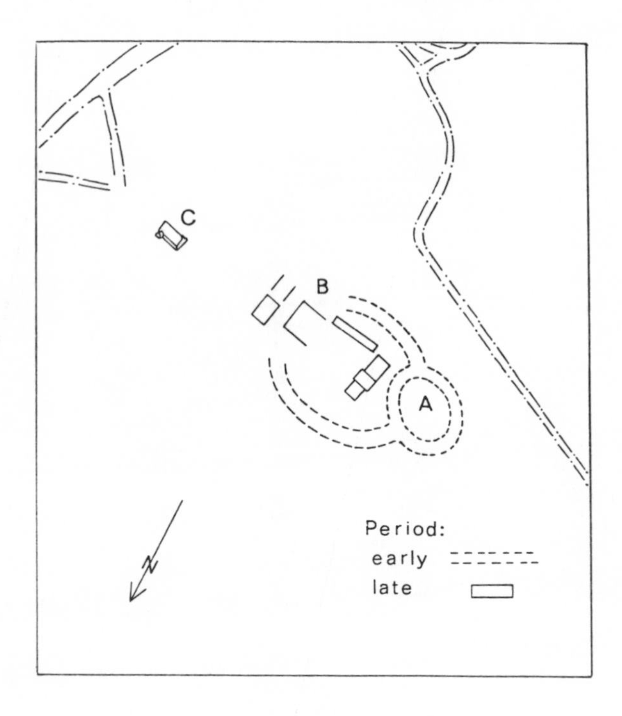

29. EARTHWORK CASTLE; CROPTON, PICKERING, NORTH YORKSHIRE

(formerly in North Riding), SE 755 893

The normal form of Norman castle is the motte and bailey, and this type was common in the period from 1066 to 1200. Strategically sited on a headland or spur overlooking Rosedale and the Vale of Pickering, Cropton Castle illustrates this type of structure well. The steep hill slopes are now tree-covered whilst the area of the castle is under grass. The mound (A) with its encircling ditch shows clearly in the low sunlight; this mound would originally have supported a timber tower some twenty feet high. On the flatter ground are the remains of a bailey building, with a rectangular enclosure showing traces of individual structures evident as low banks accentuated by rough grass (B). These were stone buildings and were part of the late medieval manor house (The Hall Garth) that replaced the timber buildings within the oval bailey or courtyard of Norman date. The village church (C), perhaps originally founded as a chapel by the Norman lord William de Stuteville, lies east of the castle with later village housing beyond.

L.A.S. Butler

Photograph by A.L. Pacitto, 5 May 1975
Reference: W. I'Anson, *Yorkshire Archaeological Journal* 22 (1912-13), pp. 344-45

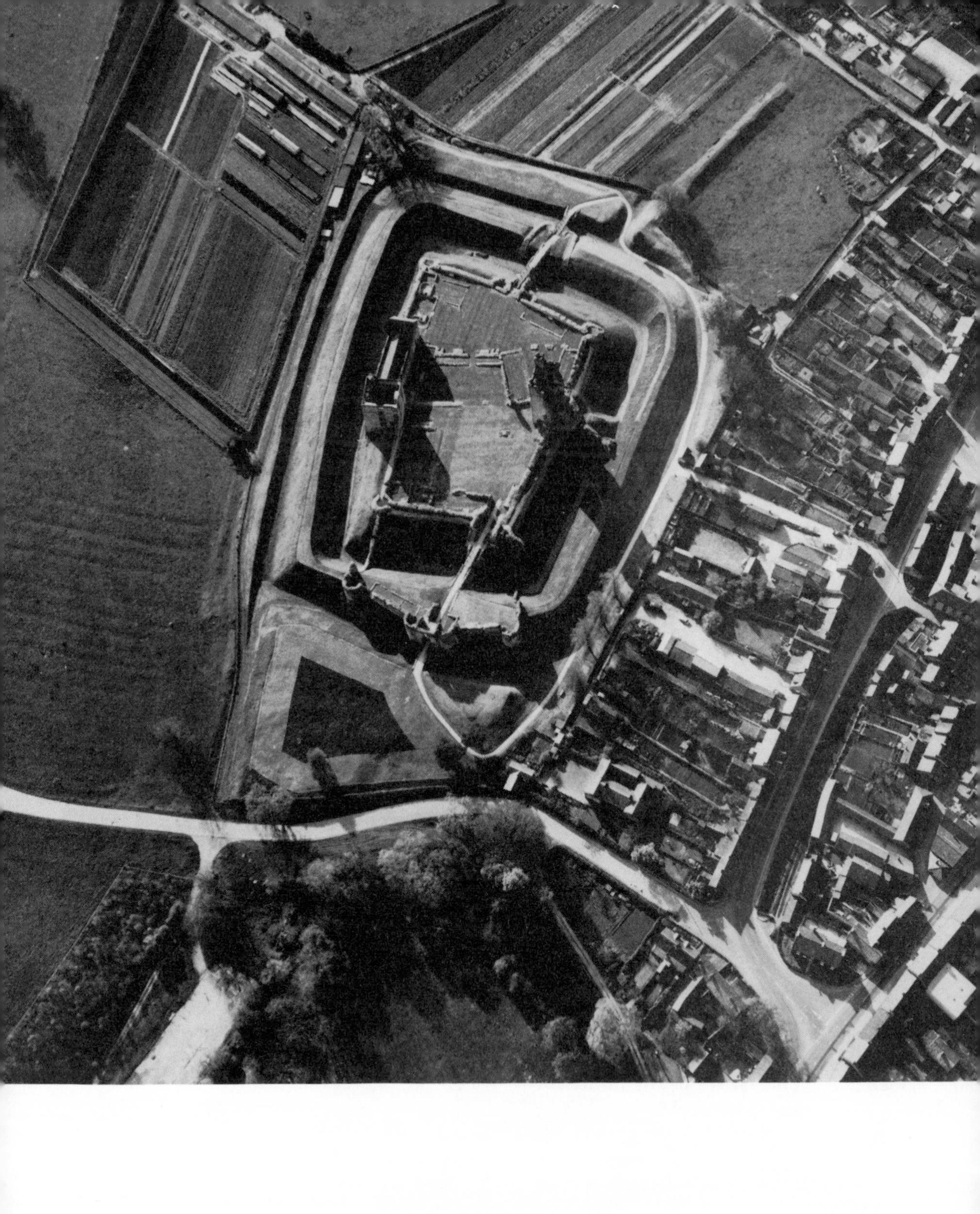

30. STONE CASTLE: HELMSLEY, NORTH YORKSHIRE

(formerly in North Riding), SE 611 836

This is an excellent example of a Norman castle which was rebuilt in stone in the thirteenth century. It continued to be occupied as a fortified residence until the Civil War siege in 1644. The castle, which stands on a ridge of limestone in central Ryedale, makes little use of water to provide its defences. Instead the garrison relied on the massive earthwork banks, which are shown well by the deep shadows cast by low sunlight.

The inner courtyard has a curtain wall and circular towers, surrounding the domestic buildings still visible as foundations. The defences on the outer circuit were built only where protection was needed for the approach bridges. The outer ditch has a counterscarp bank for most of its circuit. There is some trace of an earth dam (upper centre) which retained water in the pond for the castle's mill.

Although it stands on a site chosen by Walter l'Espec (died 1154), most of the castle now visible today is the work of the Ros family. The castle ruins stand on the western edge of the small town; the market place survives (right), partly infilled by later housing. To the west of the castle (left) the ridge and furrow of the medieval common fields can be seen in the parkland of Duncombe House.

L.A.S. Butler

Photograph by A.L. Pacitto

Reference: C.R. Peers, *Helmsley Castle* (Official Handbook)

31. BYLAND ABBEY, NORTH YORKSHIRE

(formerly in North Riding), SE 549 789

The Cistercian Abbey was founded in 1177 by a community of monks who had attempted to settle in many previous homes in Lancashire and Yorkshire. Their final site at Byland was then an island in an isolated marshy valley. Most of the Abbey buildings were completed by 1250 and the church suffered no later alterations.

The plan is the normal cloister arrangement, with the cruciform church to the north (top), the lay brothers' range (left) to the west, the chapter house (right centre) to the east and the domestic buildings of refectory, kitchens and infirmary (lower centre and right). It was this last area that received most development in the later Middle Ages, with the creation of minor courtyards surrounded by service buildings.

After the Dissolution in 1539 the Abbey was gradually robbed of its stone, and only parts of the church stand to any height. The site was cleared of tumbled stone and laid out by the office of Works from 1920 onwards.

The use of this oblique photograph enables the lay-out of the ruins to be seen clearly. On a sunny day, shadows would obscure the plan, though they might emphasize irregularities of the ground surface. In this midwinter view the unmown grass is short and shows up former watercourses and drains as dark lines. Some water lies in hollows (upper right).

L.A.S. Butler

Photograph by A.L. Pacitto, 7 February 1975

References: C.R. Peers, *Byland Abbey* (Official Handbook, 1936)

D. Knowles and J.K. St Joseph, *Monastic Sites from the Air* (Cambridge, 1952), pp. 86-89

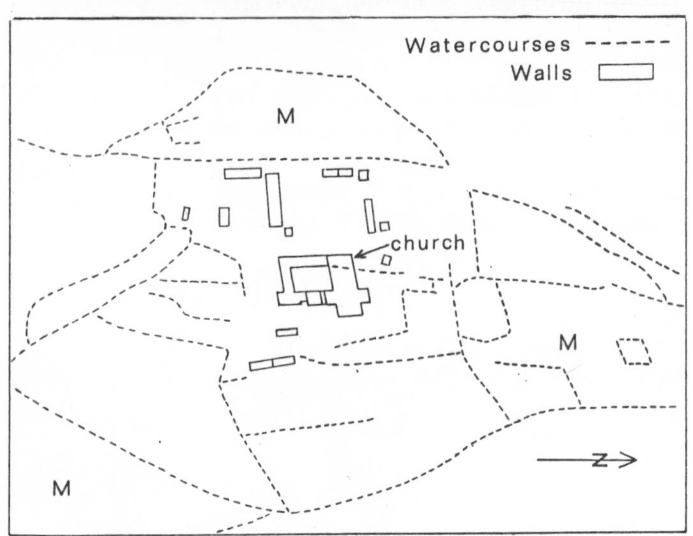
Watercourses
Walls
M
church
M
M
N

32. MEAUX ABBEY, NEAR BEVERLEY, NORTH HUMBERSIDE

(formerly in East Riding), TA 092 394

This Cistercian Abbey was founded in 1151 by William le Gros, Count of Aumale. He gave to Adam and a band of monks from Fountains a site where he had intended to build a hunting lodge, and bestowed on them extensive endowments in Holderness. The community flourished until the Black Death, which affected the house severely. It continued on a reduced level until the Dissolution in 1539, after which its buildings were robbed for material to strengthen Hull's defences.

A typical abbey comprised three zones of activity: the innermost zone of church and cloister, the outer precinct of related domestic buildings and the outermost area with supporting industrial or agricultural uses. This is well illustrated at Meaux.

At the centre was the cruciform church, dedicated in 1253 and similar in plan to Byland, and the cloister with three ranges of accommodation. To the east lay the infirmary and the abbot's lodging; to the west stood the guest houses and store sheds of the outer precinct. All these are marked by low banks which are accentuated by shadows cast in the low sunlight. Beyond the abbey on all sides are depressions marking the mill ponds and fish ponds, and the drainage channels so necessary on this low-lying site, the 'vineyard of heaven'. In some enclosures medieval ploughing is visible (M on drawing), but in the foreground is the narrow rigg and furrow typical of post-medieval cultivation.

L.A.S. Butler

Photograph by D.R. Wilson, 4 June 1970

References: P. Fergusson, *Architecture of Solitude* (1984), pp. 19, 133-36

R. Butler, Meaux Abbey', *Archaeological Journal* 141 (1984), pp. 46-48

T. Sheppard, 'Meaux Abbey', *East Riding Archaeological Society Transactions* 26 (1929), pp. 106-36

33. TADCASTER, NORTH YORKSHIRE

(formerly West Riding), SE 485 435

The small market town of Tadcaster stands beside the River Wharfe. Here the Roman town of *Calcaria* replaced the fort at Newton Kyme (19), but only slight evidence of Roman occupation has yet been found. The settlement was known as *Caelcacaestir* when Bede wrote in the 730s and as *Tathacaester* in the Anglo-Saxon Chronicle, when it described the Norse invasion of 1066. It was an important river crossing; north of the town are the earthwork remains of the Norman castle (upper centre) in the grassy field made uneven by quarrying. The church has some Norman work, though it is largely fifteenth century. The town lies on either side of High Street; the southern sector (foreground) is now occupied by breweries, but the northern sector is more domestic, with Kirkgate leading into a small triangular market. It is the northern sector that may overlie the Roman town and evidence might be found in the recently cleared central car park.

Outside the medieval core of the town, the importance of communications is shown by the early nineteenth century railway bridge on an abortive line to York. Between the two bridges the river weir shows as a white waterfall.

L.A.S. Butler

Photograph by A.J.G. Crawshaw, June 1985
Reference: *Victoria County History of Yorkshire* 2 (1912), p. 39 (castle)

34. THE CITY OF YORK

In the background is the Minster, aligned liturgically east to west, an alignment conflicting with that of the city streets around it, which reflect an earlier Roman pattern. The Minster lies within the Roman legionary fortress, the defences of which can be followed by the belt of trees at the top of the photograph, though they are now buried beneath the bank of the medieval city walls. The white tower on their line to the east (right) of the Minster is Monk Bar, the city's eastern gate.

In the foreground are York's two rivers, the Ouse (left) and the Foss (right), one of the keys to the Roman's choice of site and the city's continued prosperity. Of the two bridges visible across the Ouse, the nearer, Skeldergate Bridge, is a fine Victorian iron structure on a new site. The further is a Regency stone replacement of the medieval bridge that so fascinated the topographical painters of the city. Between the rivers is the Castle, where three magnificent eighteenth-century public buildings stand in the bailey below the thirteenth century Clifford's Tower on its Norman mound.

Three contrasting medieval church towers lie fortuitously in line between Clifford's Tower and the Minster transept, each adding to the interest of the city's street-scape, without challenging the Minster's dominance. The photograph demonstrates well how York has thankfully avoided large modern developments, and how much it still retains its medieval character of buildings small in scale, huddled along narrow streets and dominated as they have been since Norman times by the magnificent cathedral. In Roman times there was the same dominance of one building. Then, on the same site but with a different alignment, the massive great hall of the *principia* would have risen above a more ordered and regimented group of low buildings.

H.G. Ramm

Photograph by P.V. Addyman

35. FLAXTON, NORTH YORKSHIRE

(formerly in East Riding), SE 679 623

Many villages in Yorkshire developed along a single street with one or two rows of houses. It is not certain whether this was a planned development or whether it occurred accidentally. Flaxton, a small village north-east of York, shows one row of houses to the north of the village street (right), but only a few survivors or replacements of the row to the south. Beyond the huddle of housing and trees on the south row there are traces of other houses and garden banks, visible as low mounds and now incorporated in the grass of the village green; there are similar less distinct hints of former houses in the foreground.

At the back of the houses on the north row are garden plots and enclosed strip fields. Some houses have five or six strips in the former common field, a few have three or less. Whilst the influence of the ridge and furrow is strong on the north, it is absent on the south. This suggests that either the land had been long under grass as common grazing or that the ridge and furrow had been so long ploughed out by cross ploughing that it did not influence later field shape or division. Narrow field lanes between the hedges give access to the village lands.

L.A.S. Butler

Photograph by D.N. Riley, 25 July 1984
Reference: B.K. Roberts, *Rural Settlement in Britain* (1977), pp. 117-58

36. DESERTED MEDIEVAL VILLAGE, COWLAM, NORTH HUMBERSIDE

(formerly in East Riding), SE 965 657

The medieval villages on the chalk wolds suffered from late medieval depopulation and desertion, mainly due to the switch from labour-intensive arable to pastoral farming. At this site the earthworks of former houses and garden plots (tofts and crofts) show clearly. Cowlam was deserted in about 1680, though in 1674 there were fourteen resident householders.

The village comprises four main streets, three of them deserted. The east street (foreground) has at least twelve houses, marked by shallow depressions, set within a boundary bank. The north street (centre) has ten or more houses, some of which show as depressions and others as rectangular banks. Most houses have an inner garden and an outer plot, some containing ponds and a few subdivided by low walls. To the left of the village street (showing as a sunken hollow, partly used by the modern track) are more houses and gardens. The south street (left) has been much damaged by recent ploughing and only a few traces of its house and garden banks show. Patches of bare chalk form white marks. The west street is occupied by the modern farm buildings (upper left).

Low evening sunlight enables the shadows thrown by the village earthworks to be seen clearly. Surrounding them are the thin lines of medieval ploughing, creating ridge and furrow patterns. The view is from the north-east.

L.A.S. Butler

Photograph by D.R. Wilson, 13 May 1968
Reproduced by permission of the Cambridge University Committee for Aerial Photography

References: M.W. Beresford and J.K. St Joseph, *Medieval England: An Aerial Survey* (2nd edn, Cambridge, 1979), pp. 124-26
C. Hayfield, *Cowlam Deserted Village: Excavations by T.C.M. Brewster 1971/72* (East Riding Archaeological Research Committee, forthcoming)

36A. COWLAM FOURTEEN YEARS LATER

This is the same site viewed from the south-west, seen after destruction caused by ploughing in 1972. The modern track which was so prominent in the 1968 photograph is less noticeable. The ploughing up of white chalk has produced very clear soil marks on the boundary banks of gardens, while individual houses show as solid white rectangles, either revealing the chalk platforms on which the houses were placed or indicating rubble banks formed by the collapse of chalk block walls. The village streets show as grey lines between the house frontage. The soil marks of the ridge and furrow are far less prominent than those of the medieval houses.

Amid the blocks of modern farm buildings, the village church (centre foreground) can be seen aligned to the medieval south street. It is a building of 1852 replacing the medieval church, but still with a Norman font. The Manor Farm now dates from the early nineteenth-century agricultural improvement, and is protected by shelter belts of trees from the winter winds and snow drifts.

L.A.S. Butler

Photograph by D.N. Riley, 5 March 1982

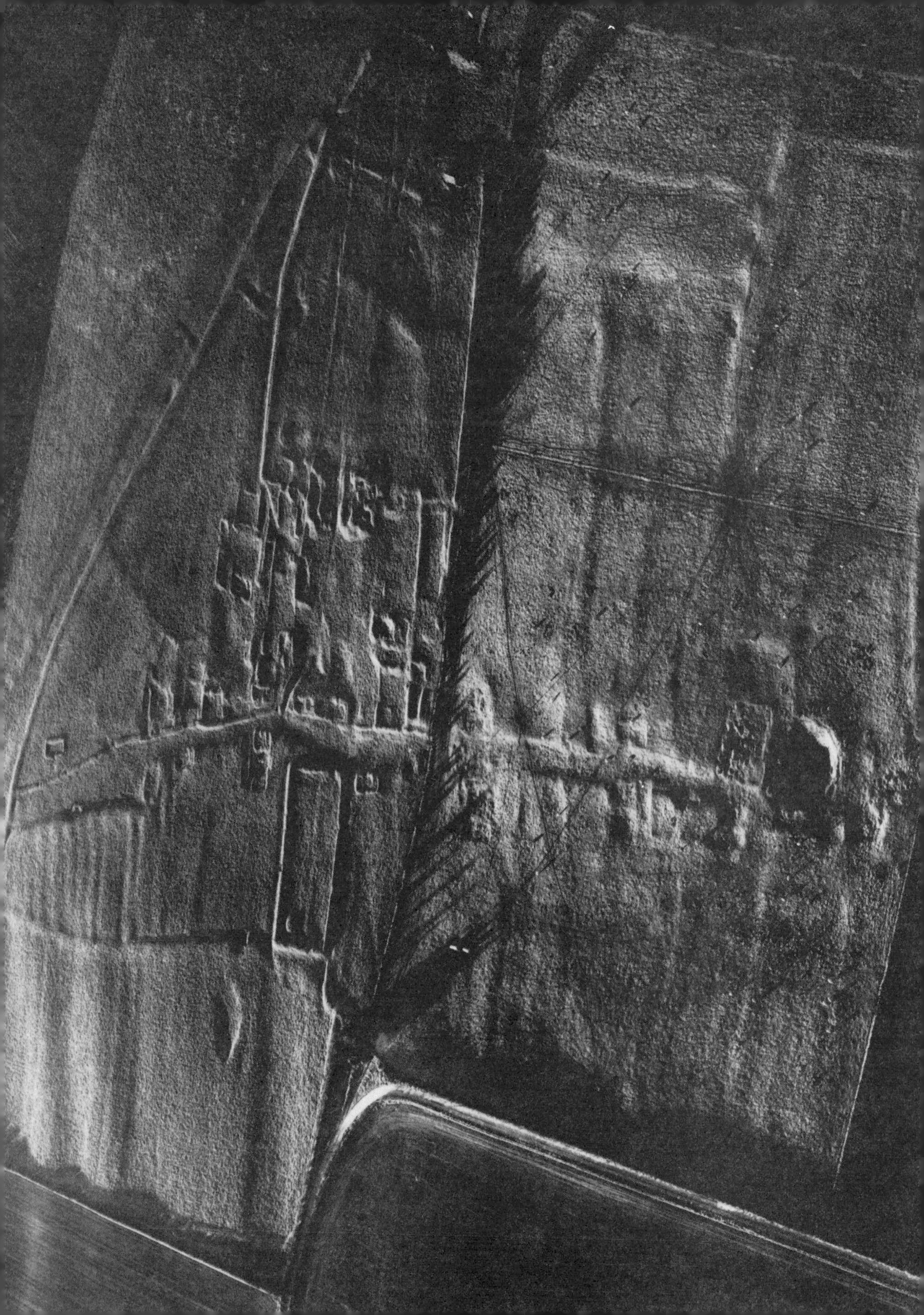

37. DESERTED MEDIEVAL VILLAGE: ARGHAM, NORTH HUMBERSIDE

(formerly in East Riding), TA 113 714

This settlement was grouped along a single street. The surviving remains, shown clearly by low sunlight, are in two contrasting forms. In the field in the foreground, formerly ploughed for a short period, the buildings on either side of the sunken way show as depressions, while their garden banks are slight ridges with rectangular outlines. The prominent depression (lower centre) is a chalk pit or quarry. Without excavation one cannot be sure that the depressions are houses; they may be cattle yards with raised house platforms alongside them.

In the more distant field the remains of medieval and later houses are better preserved. Highlights on the raised lines of their walls are accentuated by dark shadows. There are a variety of farm buildings either side of the street. The village boundary is evident (left), with a pond or chalk pit beyond. To the right of the photograph the village spreads with a series of paddocks and the long mound of an artificial rabbit warren. A prehistoric linear earthwork, the Argham Dyke, runs past the site in a straight line (centre top to mid right); it was used as a road in medieval times.

The village was deserted by the eighteenth century. The use of winter sunlight to emphasize low earthworks is enhanced by the close cropped grass—compare the lack of detail on plate 4, which shows a site under long grass. Livestock can be seen grazing in the field (base).

L.A.S. Butler

Photograph by D.R. Wilson, 9 December 1976
Reproduced by permission of the Cambridge University Committee for Aerial Photography
Reference: M.W. Beresford, 'The Lost Villages of Yorkshire', *Yorkshire Archaeological Journal* 38 (1952), pp. 4-70 (see p. 50)

38. MONASTIC GRANGE: NEW LEYS FARM, RIEVAULX, NORTH YORKSHIRE

(formerly in North Riding), SE 582 865

This monastic farm or grange lies on a headland formed by steep-sided tributary valleys of the River Rye. Originally Newlass or New Laithes was an out settlement of Helmsley, but the settlement had been granted to Rievaulx and had become a grange by 1301. During the sixteenth century, if not before, it was a specialist sheep-rearing farm. At the dissolution of the Abbey in 1539 there was 'the grange, the great sheephouse, the rabbit warren and a third building'.

In the field near the left arm of the ravine there are a long rectangular building that might be a barn and an irregular zig-zag bank that could be the rabbit warren. Within the same field there is clear evidence of ridge and furrow cultivation belonging to the earlier hamlet.

In the right hand field there is a squarish enclosure containing rectangular buildings; these might have been the sheephouse with a protected lambing yard. Two buildings lie below it on the slope. Near the top of the photograph in the same field are the remains of the farm or grange, but there are also traces of other buildings that may represent the earlier pre-Cistercian settlement. A quarry for limestone lies near the second ravine (upper right).

Evening sunlight from the west throws up strong shadows both of the slight earthworks and of the hedgerow trees. The ravines are in deep shadow.

L.A.S. Butler

Photograph by North Yorkshire County Council Planning Department (R.F. White), 23 July 1984

Reference: M.W. Beresford and J.K. St Joseph, *Medieval England: an Aerial Survey*, 2nd edn (Cambridge, 1979), pp. 160-61

39. OPEN FIELDS ENCLOSED: MIDDLETON NEAR PICKERING, NORTH YORKSHIRE

(formerly in North Riding), SE 776 845

Medieval villages were often surrounded by unhedged or 'open' fields cultivated by all the villagers working together. Such arable land was divided into three or four great fields in which the crops were sown in rotation, with one field left fallow resting unsown for a year.

When the open fields were enclosed in the eighteenth or early nineteenth century, new field boundaries were created and new permanent roads replaced the unmade tracks meandering around the furlong boundaries or headlands. Some villages, such as Middleton, north-west of Pickering, were conservative in the method of enclosure. This view from the south-west shows how the new hedges follow the gently curving outline of the former strips. In some fields the actual ridge and furrow evidence of former ploughing can be seen. The fields in the lower left corner of the photograph are in Aislaby township, where a similar sequence of enclosure was followed.

All the fields are under grass or cereal, some recently harvested. The features are showing as shadows accentuated by evening sunlight.

L.A.S. Butler

Photograph by North Yorkshire County Council (R.F. White), 23 July 1984

Reference: M.W. Beresford and J.K. St Joseph, *Medieval England: An Aerial Survey* (Cambridge, 1958), pp. 121-22 (view from south-east in 1952)

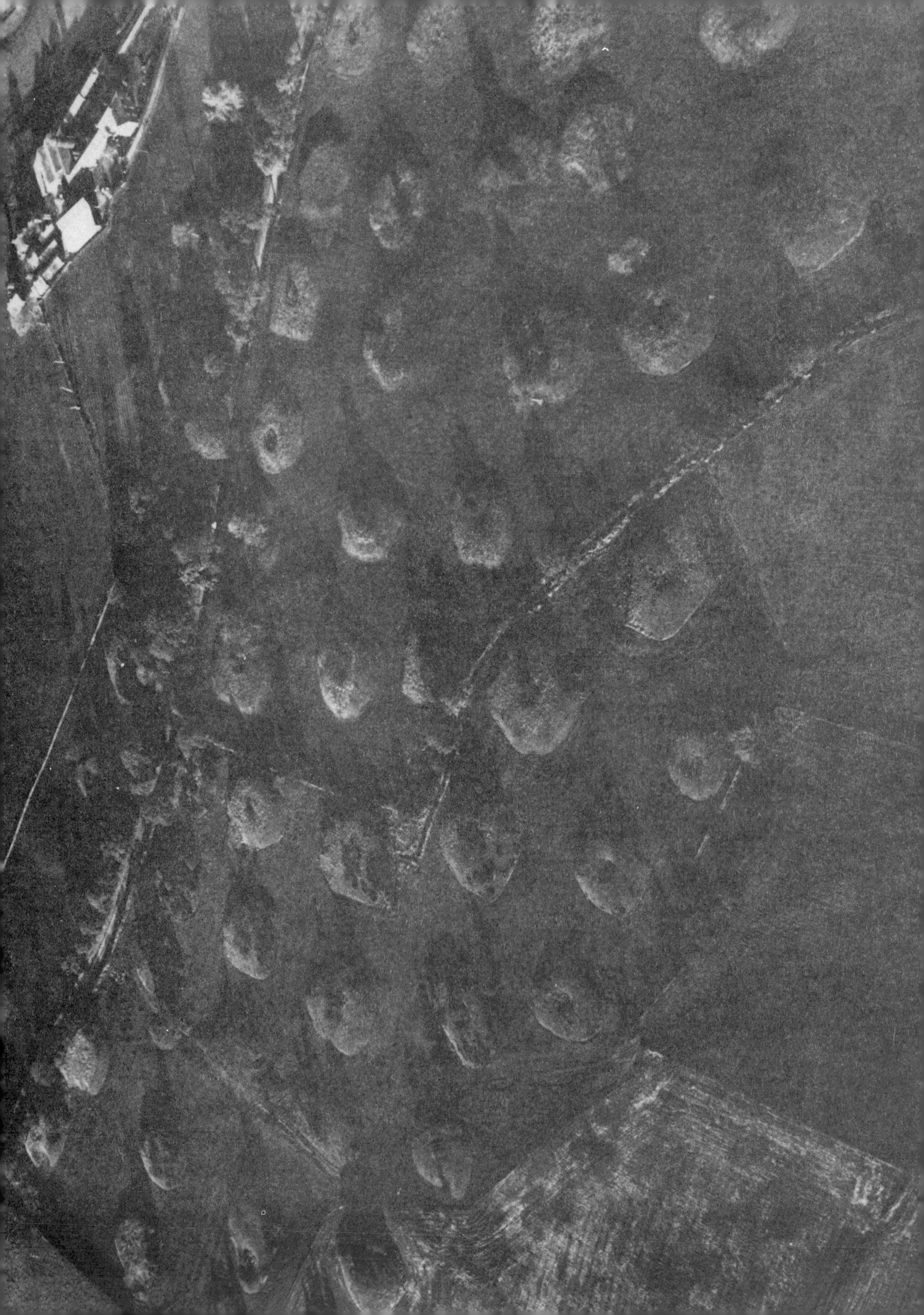

40. IRONSTONE MINES: BENTLEY GRANGE, EMLEY, WEST YORKSHIRE

(formerly in West Riding), SE 970 738

The mounds with central pits are typical of many over the Coal Measures of West and South Yorkshire, representing the spoil from underground ironstone mines. Those seen here are all that survive from a much larger group which formerly extended to the north (top of photograph) and the west (left). Thought to remain from well-documented monastic iron working at Bentley Grange (upper right), the mounds are probably the result of the extensive iron smelting activities in southern Yorkshire from the sixteenth century onwards. The ridge and furrow cultivation which surrounds and runs beneath the mounds on the left probably relates to the farming activities of the monks. A detailed survey of the vicinity has revealed at least three phases of activity earlier than the mounds, all probably connected with the iron working grange, which belonged to Byland Abbey (31).

S.A. Moorhouse

Photograph by West Yorkshire Archaeology Service (R.E. Yarwood), 11 December 1980

References: M.L. Faull, and S.A. Moorhouse (eds.), *West Yorkshire: an Archaeological Survey to AD 1500* (Wakefield, 1981), pp. 792-93
M.W. Beresford, and J.K. St Joseph, *Medieval England: An Aerial Survey* (2nd edn, Cambridge, 1979), p. 256

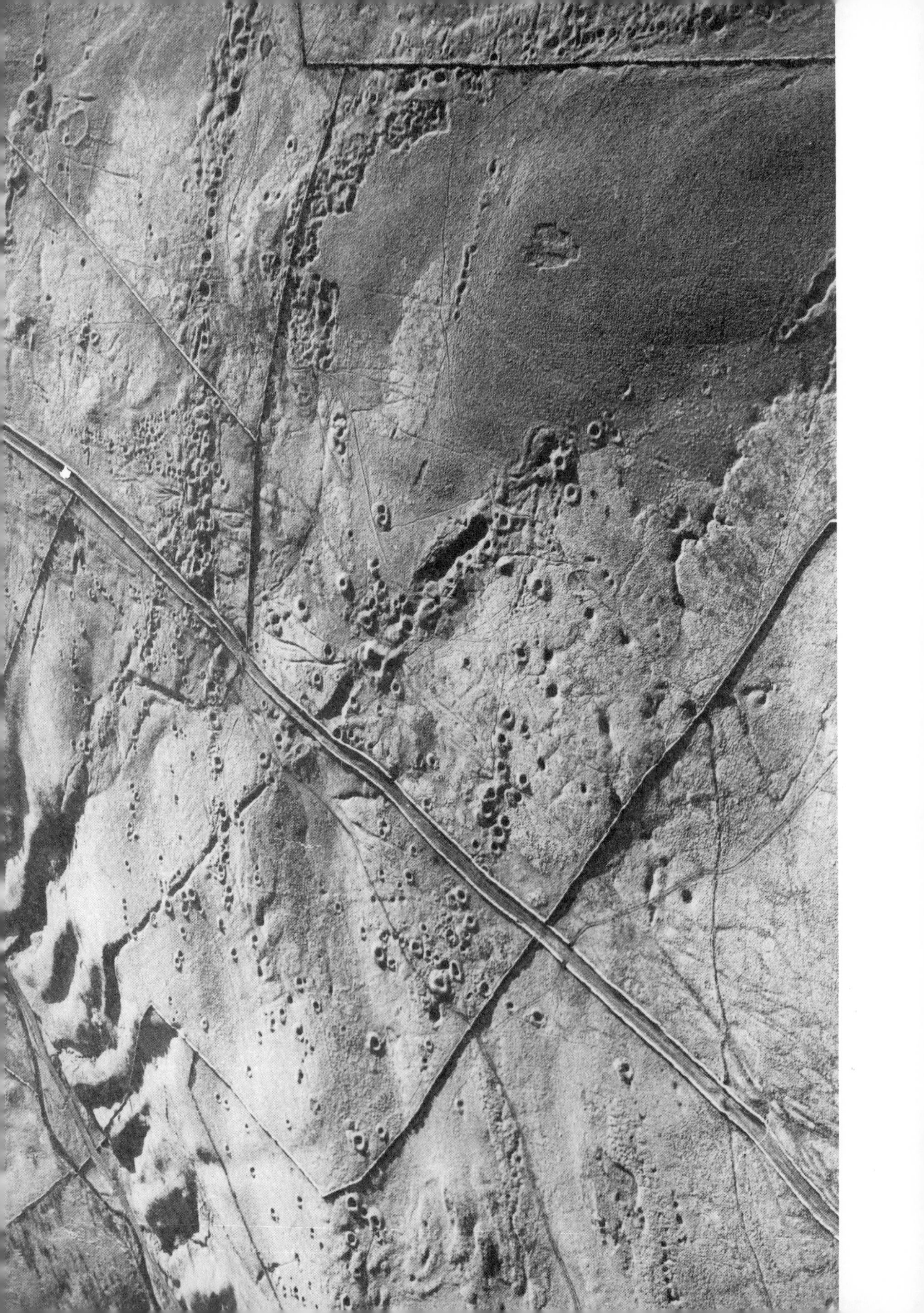

41. LEAD MINES: CAM PASTURE, KETTLEWELL, NORTH YORKSHIRE

(formerly in West Riding), SE 970 738

Cam Pasture, north of Kettlewell, is a typical piece of moorland scarred by many centuries of lead mining. The crater-like depressions follow the outcropping lead seams, hence the number of obvious lines of depressions. The technique of lead mining altered little through the ages. Roman mining is known in the vicinity, while the area was mined during the Middle Ages. There are specific references to lead mining at Kettlewell between 1502 and 1513, and the area certainly provided lead ore for the famous Kettlewell Mill on the Cam Gill Beck during the post-medieval period and until 1943, when it was demolished. It is therefore likely that many centuries of lead mining activity are illustrated. In the upper right corner of the photograph is seen a small banked or walled enclosure, perhaps an ancient feature (compare 10).

S. Moorhouse

Photograph by D.N. Riley, 6 December 1983
Reference: R.T. Clough, *The Lead Smelting Mills of the Yorkshire Dales* (Keighley, 1952)

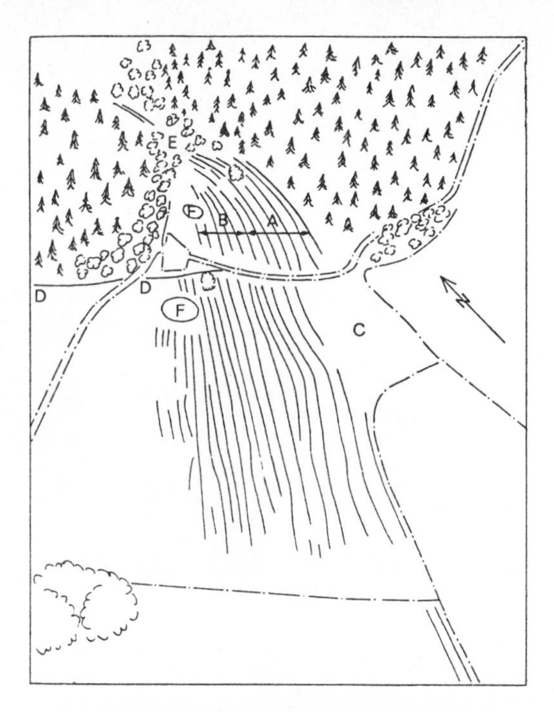

42. THE COCKMOOR DYKES, SNAINTON, NORTH YORKSHIRE

(formerly in North Riding), SE 914 868

These astonishing parallel dykes (banks and ditches), apparently unique in Britain, are situated in an area with many prehistoric linear earthworks. They present some difficult problems of interpretation. There are two main components. The first is the six major dykes on the right (A), which have banks some 6 ft (2 m) high above the ditch bottoms. According to the 1954 edition of the Ordnance Survey 6 inches to 1 mile map, these dykes continued nearly 2 miles (3000 m) southwards along the side of Wyedale. Now they are much destroyed, including the part on area C, where banks and ditches are shown on the old OS maps. They are similar to other large prehistoric multiple dykes, such as those seen on the Weaverthorpe photograph (12).

The second component is the smaller dykes on the left (B), 1.5 to 6 ft (0.5 to 2 m) in height, which can be seen by field evidence to be later in date and do not continue southwards. They seem to be post-medieval, for they stop at the medieval road DD, which cuts through the major dykes (A); and it is probably that they were made after 1707, because in a boundary survey of that year the whole complex is called the Snainton Six Dykes. Various explanations of their purpose have been proposed, though none is entirely convincing. One suggestion is that the banks were made for the burrows of rabbits from the huge warren which formerly occupied the area to the west, but if so they are unlike the single mounds of banks made for this purpose elsewhere. A track which enters the dykes by a hollow way at E certainly made use of them, but they cannot be successive routes of this track because some are interrupted by the barrows FF. Field work and documentary study can take us so far; perhaps only an excavation will reveal the truth.

D.A. Spratt

Photograph by D. Powlesland, 14 September 1981

Reference: B.G. Drummond, and D.A. Spratt, 'Cockmoor Dykes and Rabbit Warrening', *Ryedale Historian* 12 (1984), pp. 22-30

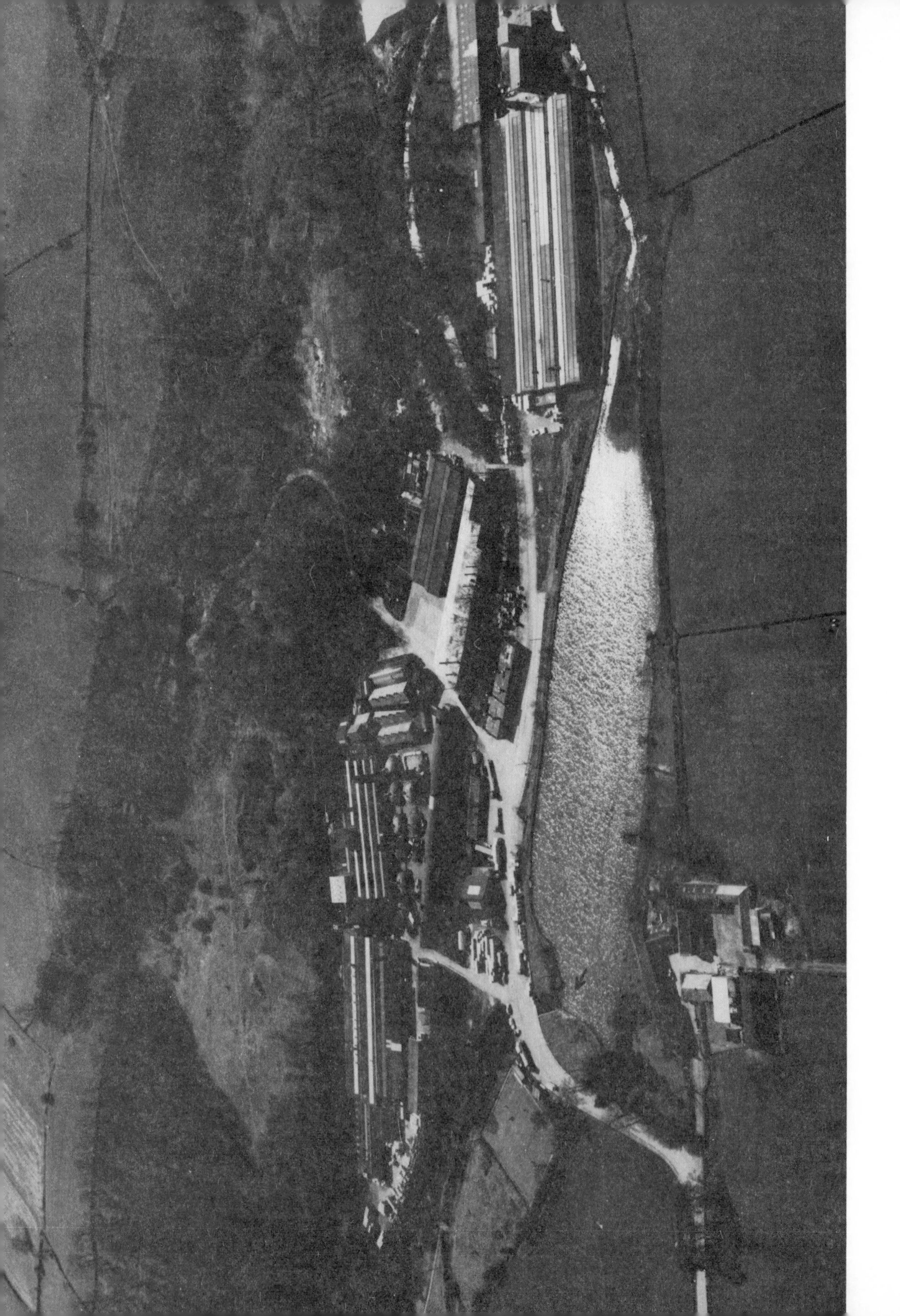

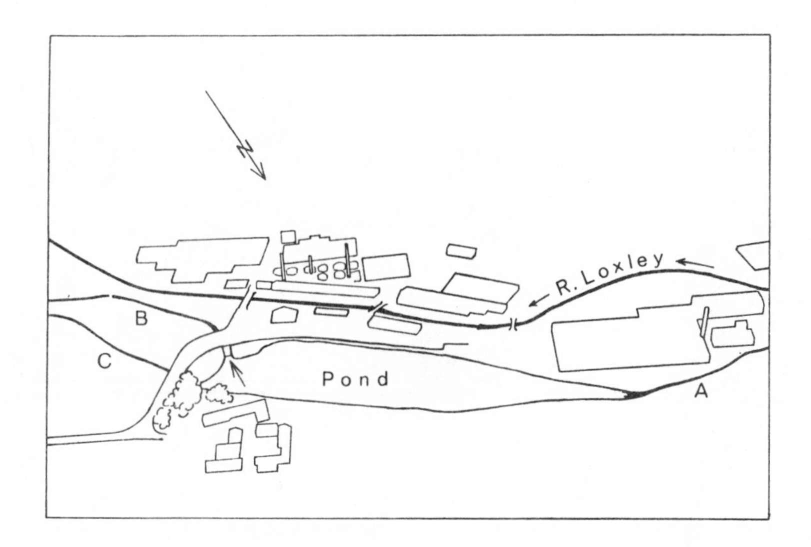

43. THE OLD WHEEL ON THE RIVER LOXLEY, BRADFIELD, SOUTH YORKSHIRE

(formerly West Riding), SK 296 898

Water power was the main motive force of early industry, and in the Sheffield area all the numerous streams were exploited to the full. The Old Wheel was one of several small works that formerly depended on the River Loxley. Water is diverted from the river by a weir outside the picture to the right, and still reaches the pond by a long goit or channel (A). A stone-lined pit for water wheels can be seen in the dam (see arrow at left of pond). From it, the tail race (B) runs down the valley, to join the stream carrying the overflow of the pond (C) and supply water power to the next works about a quarter mile (400 m) downstream, outside the photograph to the left.

In the late seventeenth century there was a cutler's grinding shop at the Old Wheel. Early in the nineteenth century Samuel Newbould developed the site, enlarging the pond and building a tilt-forge for working steel. There were then four water wheels, two for the tilt-hammers, one for the furnace blower and one for cutler's grinding wheels. The site of the tilt-forge is under the road beyond the pond. The buildings were badly damaged in the Great Sheffield Flood of 1864, which was caused by the bursting of a dam upstream, but they were afterwards rebuilt.

By 1861 Thomas Wragg was getting ganister from the hillside (background) to make refractory (heat-resisting) materials for the steel industry in Sheffield. He later took over the Old Wheel, using its water power for grinding the ganister. The plant still makes refractory bricks and special shapes for furnace linings, which are sent all over the world.

D.N. Riley

Photograph by D.N. Riley, 30 April 1977

Reference: W.T. Miller, *The Water Mills of Sheffield* (Pawson & Brailsford, Sheffield, 1936), pp. 81-82

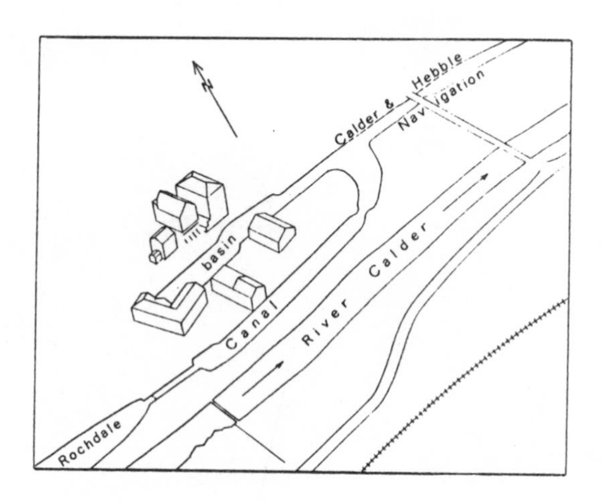

44. CANALS: SOWERBY BRIDGE, WEST YORKSHIRE

(formerly in West Riding), SE 065 237

The late eighteenth century was a great period for canal building, during which the Leeds-Liverpool Canal Act was passed in 1770. The impressive basin with its warehouse complex was made as the western terminus of the Calder and Hebble Navigation, and was later joined by the Rochdale Canal, completed in 1804, to link Manchester and Rochdale with the towns of the Calder valley. The canals provided an easy form of communication for transporting bulk commodities across the Pennines for use in the rapidly developing textile industry of the towns of Lancashire and the West Riding. The subsequent expansion of the railway network at the expense of the canals caused the decline in importance of warehouse and repair facilities such as those at Sowerby Bridge during the later nineteenth century. Recent years have seen changing fortunes, for the complex now houses a restaurant, marina and boat building and repair yards. Beyond the left edge of the photograph lies a unique sequence of riverside mills and textile buildings dating from the late medieval period, with an underground network of goits and water courses, emphasizing the important role that this part of West Yorkshire played in the history of the textile industry.

S.A. Moorhouse

Photograph by West Yorkshire Archaeology Service (R.E. Yarwood), 12 November 1980

45. STOCKSBRIDGE WORKS, SHEFFIELD, SOUTH YORKSHIRE

(formerly West Riding), SK 273 985

At the end of the eighteenth century a small mill was built here to take advantage of the water power available from the Little Don River, another of the smaller streams of the Sheffield area. There still remains a stone marked I.S. Denton 1794, the name of the first owner, Jonathan Denton, and Sarah his wife. The mill passed through the hands of several proprietors and was used for a variety of trades, including cotton spinning, and had a chequered history, until in 1841 (this date was previously thought to have been 1842) a new tenant arrived, Samuel Fox, who had previously for a short time been one of the partners in a wire-drawing business at a mill in the Rivelin Valley, yet another of the small Sheffield streams.

Under Samuel Fox progress was rapid. By about 1847 some of his steel wire was being used to make umbrella frames, and in 1852 he patented the 'Paragon' frame, strong and light, the prototype of all modern umbrellas. He bought the mill in 1851, and in the next decade made a fortune from special wire for crinolines, the short-lived fashion for ladies' dresses of that name. About 1860 the works began steelmaking, an event which has shaped the future of the valley ever since. Samuel Fox died in 1887, but his memory is still alive in the neighbourhood and stories of him still last. A well-known one concerns his foreman Joseph Hayward, who invented the 'Paragon' frame: it is said that a workman told Fox that Hayward was asleep, and received the reply, 'Thee go and mind thi work, he's worth more to me asleep than thou art wakken!'

The two tall stone buildings in the foreground of the photograph (*marked by arrows*) were built by Fox in the mid nineteenth century to house the plant producing wire and umbrellas. They were tall and narrow so that full advantage could be taken of natural light from their windows. Now that umbrella frame-making has ceased and wire-drawing has moved away, the old buildings house technical and administrative staff serving the steel-works that extend along the valley beyond both the background and the foreground of the photograph.

The following dates have been milestones in the history of steelmaking at Stocksbridge: 1862, Samuel Fox granted one of the first licences for the Bessemer process of bulk steelmaking; 1899, open hearth steelmaking introduced; 1929, electric steelmaking plant first installed. In recent years there has been much capital investment in advanced methods of making and processing steel, and the works, now operated by Stocksbridge Engineering Steels, is one of the world leaders in high grade alloy steel production.

Although Fox's umbrella frames, famous in Victorian England, are a thing of the past at the works, other specialized steel products—wire, cold rolled strip, springs, stainless steel sheet—are made in the Stocksbridge valley or in eastern Sheffield at successor companies under separate ownership. Part of the strip building is seen in the left foreground. Innovation, high quality and continuity have been factors of great importance in the history of industry here for nearly 150 years.

D.N. Riley

Photograph by D.N. Riley, 27 November 1987

Reference: H. Stansfield, *Samuel Fox and Company Limited 1842-1967* (booklet published by the company in 1967 on the occasion of its 125th anniversary)

46. VICTORIAN PLANNING: SALTAIRE, SHIPLEY, WEST YORKSHIRE

(formerly in West Riding), SE 138 380

Sir Titus Salt started building his model textile community on the southern banks of the River Aire (left margin of photograph) in about 1850, a combination that gave the name Saltaire. The purpose was to provide not only adequate housing for his workers, within what was then a rural setting, but also social, religious, medical and educational facilities, even for those retired from the mill service. On this photograph, looking east, we see Salt's mill (left centre) with its excellent transport services, the Leeds–Liverpool Canal (built 1773-8) and the Midland Railway (1847). The imposing facade of the mill faces across Victoria Road up to the avenue approaching the entrance portico of the fine church. Further along Victoria Road is the grand entrance to Victoria Hall (centre right), opposite which, on the other side of the road, is the symmetrically planned school. Behind the school is the orderly mill-workers' housing (right foreground). At the southern end of Victoria Road (off the picture to the right) are the hospital and quadrangle of alms houses, while further terrace houses lie to the west (off, lower right). The park (lower left), with purpose built pavilion, is across the river. The iron bridge which originally gave access from the village to the park has been demolished, and the bridge at the end of Victoria Road is its modern replacement. Two unusual features of Saltaire are that the streets are named after Christian names of either the royal family or that of Sir Titus Salt, while the builder's religious beliefs banned a public house from the complex, a situation that still persists today.

S.A. Moorhouse

Photograph by West Yorkshire Archaeology Service (R.E. Yarwood), 12 November 1985
Reference: J. Reynolds, *The Great Paternalist: Sir Titus Salt and the Growth of Bradford* (London, 1983)

47. TERRACED HOUSING: HOLBECK, LEEDS, WEST YORKSHIRE

(formerly in West Riding), SE 296 309

Large areas of regularly laid out back-to-back terrraced houses are typical of most industrial centres in West Yorkshire. They were the product of an expanding economy and a matching growth or population. Much of the housing was the result of speculative builders buying up plots of land and developing terraces one at a time, which led not only to irregular groups of streets, but also to streets being different in detail. This massive expansion of urban workers' housing took place during the late nineteenth and early twentieth centuries, but was in decline by the time of the First World War. The characteristic grouping of back-to-back houses seen on this photograph is in Holbeck township, south of Leeds. Looking north-west, Dewsbury Road crosses the lower right hand corner, while the main road from centre top to base is Tempest Road. Typically, such complexes contain a church and a school. On the left is East End Park, an early green belt between Holbeck and Beeston.

S.A. Moorhouse

Photograph by West Yorkshire Archaeology Service (R.E. Yarwood), 24 October 1983
Reference: L. Dewhurst, *Worker's Housing in West Yorkshire* (HMSO, 1985)

48. CARLTON TOWERS, NEAR SNAITH, NORTH YORKSHIRE

(formerly in East Riding), SE 650 238

Carlton Towers, the home of Lord Beaumont (the present Duke of Norfolk), stands amid parkland on a slight rise above the Humber levels near the confluence of the River Ouse and Aire. This photograph is taken from the south-west. There are three periods of building work in the house: the early seventeenth-century domestic block (lower left), the Georgian wing of 'state apartments' (right) and the three Victorian towers whose shadows are cast beyond the house. All that is now visible externally has been concealed in an extravagant Gothic cloak of cement casing, built by the younger Pugin for Henry, ninth Lord Beaumont, in 1869–74. An even more ambitious scheme would have added a Gothic keep with a grand staircase, a cruciform chapel wing to the east and a great Hall of the Barons to the south. Financial difficulties prevented progress on these buildings. North of the house is the walled kitchen garden and the greenhouses. To the west is the Edwardian formal garden in the French style.

The parkland shows little trace of the village fields predating the house. Instead there is random tree planting to enhance the view to the south and south-east. A shelter belt protects the house and gardens from the east and north winds. A screen of trees hides the house from the village with its few estate cottages. The main road from Snaith to Selby passes through the village.

L.A.S. Butler

Photograph by D.N. Riley, 2 October 1984
Reference: M. Girouard, *The Victorian Country House* (Oxford, 1971), pp. 150-54

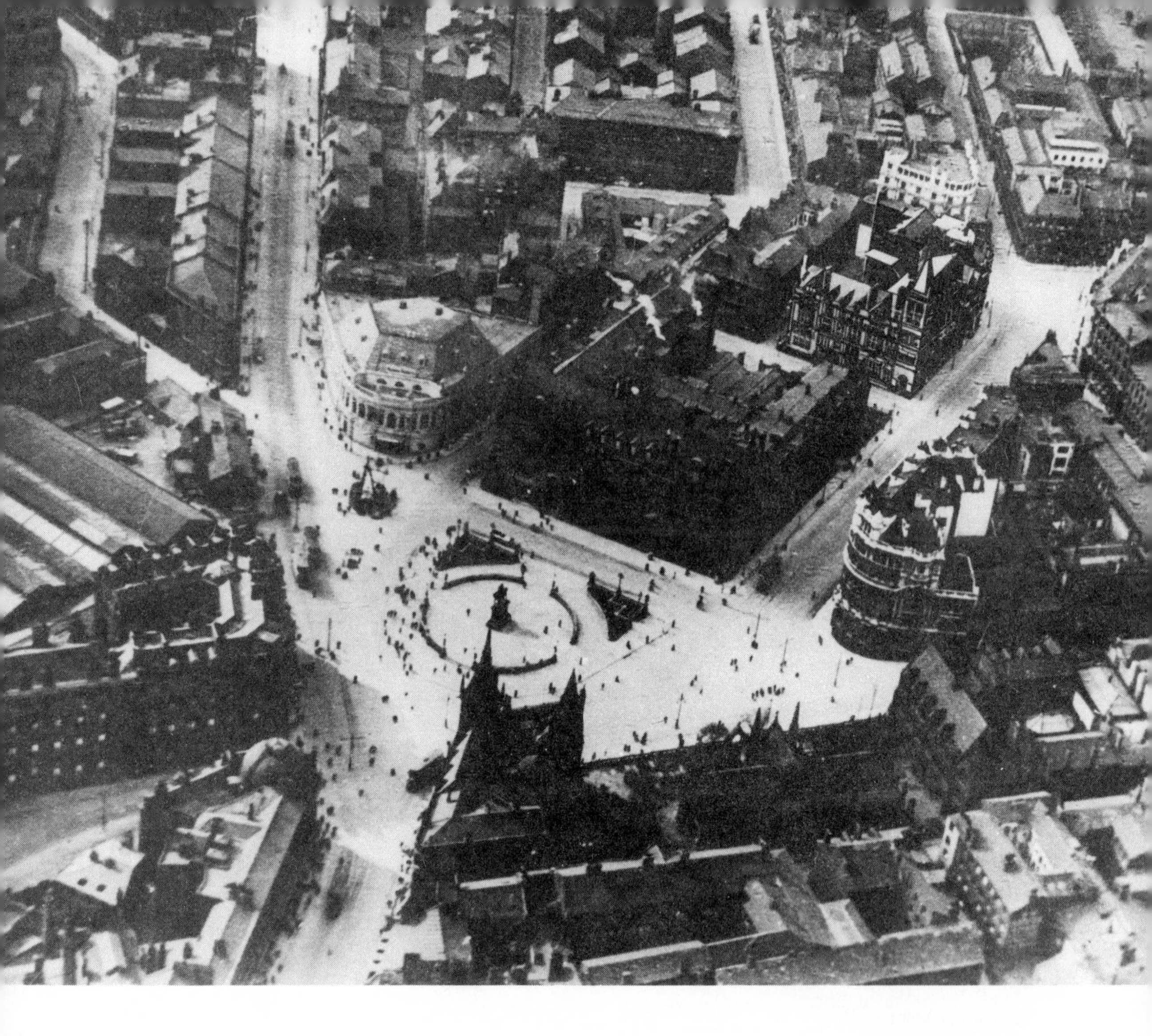

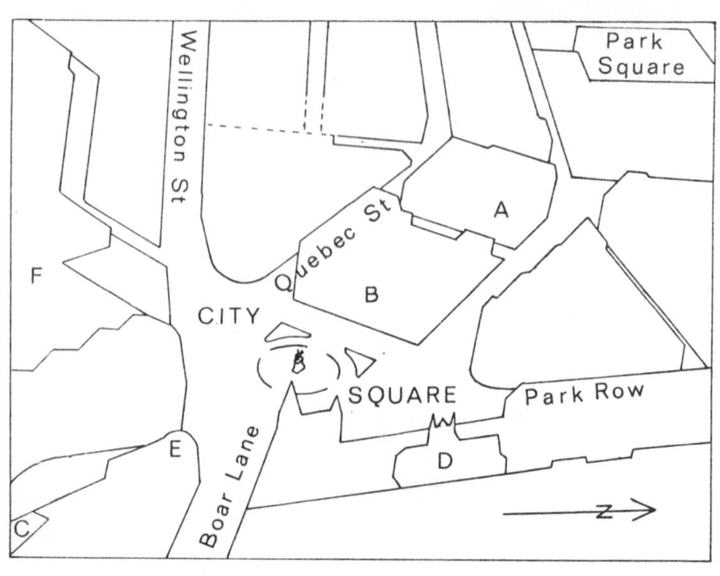

Park Square
Wellington St
Quebec St
A
B
F
CITY
SQUARE
Park Row
E
D
Boar Lane
C
N

49. LEEDS CITY SQUARE IN 1929

This photograph, taken in 1929, may have been intended for publicity by the then Yorkshire Penny Bank, (A) since its florid architectural features have been touched up. The bank replaced the Leeds General Infirmary of 1771. The central feature, however, remains City Square, actually a triangle. It was initiated by the Council in 1889 when the Coloured Cloth Hall of 1758 and its fore-buildings were purchased and the site cleared. From 1896 a large Post Office (B) occupied most of the Hall site: its large, dark facade can be seen here on the further side of the central open space, named City Square in 1893 to commemorate the recent elevation of the borough to a city. Civic pride is also represented by a statue of the Black Prince who was then (mistakenly) thought to have imported textile skills to the town; he is surrounded by a low, circular balustrade and eight female figures with lamps; statues of four (male) Leeds worthies were placed on the two higher balustrades that conceal the entrances to a subterranean public lavatory for each sex.

The creation of City Square was the final stage in the westward movement of the town's centre of gravity. Unlike most medieval towns, Leeds previously had no central urban open space since its market place was the broad main street, Briggate. Boar Lane, bottom left, terminated here on the edge of the manorial park, and the bottom left-hand corner of this photograph just manages to catch the chimneys and roof of out-buildings to the former manor house (now encased in the Scarbrough Hotel (C), Bishopgate St.). The first invasion of the park was Mill Hill Chapel and graveyard (1674), replaced in 1848 by Pugin's Gothic building (D) of which the small twin spires can be seen bottom centre. The larger spires to its left are those of a secular edifice, the Royal Exchange (1875), and above it, across Park Row, are the Norwich Union Insurance offices.

On the opposite side of Boar Lane is the rotunda roof (E) of the former Yorkshire District Bank (1836). Long straight roofs, left centre, mark the Leeds New Station (F) with its blind frontage covered by the five-storey Railway Offices, emphasizing the absence of any public open space here when they were built in 1864. Soon after this photograph was taken they would be demolished for the Queen's Hotel. The most recent building shown here, on the left of the Post Office, is the Majestic Cinema with its facade curving round into Wellington Street and Quebec Street. Beyond it, and also centre right, are blocks of warehouses built 1830-50 for the display of textiles and clothing manufactured in mills outside the town centre.

In the top right-hand corner, the Georgian houses around the grassy space of Park Square and the long facades of East Parade and Park Place remain from the town's first residential West End, initiated in 1768 but not completed before 1815. By 1929 the only residents in the whole area of the photograph would have been caretakers, whether of banks, warehouses, insurance offices and shops (the latter only in Boar Lane) or of the dentist, doctors and solicitors who worked by day in the Georgian terraces but by evening had to be sought in the suburbs and beyond. There seem to be no cars, although the photograph was taken in the afternoon (this is indicated by the shadows), but six electric trams are in view.

M.W. Beresford

The photograph, reproduced by kind permission of the Thoresby Society, was taken by a Rochdale photographer, whose name unfortunately has not been recorded

References: G. Black, 'City Square and Colonel Harding', *Publications of the Thoresby Society* 54 (1975), pp. 106-12

R.G. Wilson, *Gentlemen Merchants* (1971), ch. 9

CONTRIBUTORS TO THIS VOLUME

Authors (and main subjects described)

T.G. Manby (Prehistoric sites)
H.G. Ramm (Romano-British sites)
L.A.S. Butler (Medieval sites)
S.A. Moorhouse (Post-Medieval and later sites)
D.N. Riley (Introduction)
R.K. Morris
D.A. Spratt
M.W. Beresford

Photographers

Based in Yorkshire

P.V. Addyman
P. Chadwick
A.J.G. Crawshaw
A.L. Pacitto
D.N. Riley
R.F. White
R.E. Yarwood

Cambridge University

J.K. St Joseph
D.R. Wilson

The Yorkshire Archaeological Society has been aided in its part of the production of this book by grants received from the West Yorkshire Joint Committee for Grants to Voluntary Bodies, the Robert Kiln Charitable Trust and English Heritage.